A

MW00884074

Saflat

David Prothero

ISBN:1540783650
ISBN-9781540783653

i

DEDICATION

This book is Dedicated to:
My late Father, Alun who taught me that I could do anything I chose to do.
My Mother, Mary who gave me my Joie de Vivre
My brother, Martin who understood what we wanted to do and gave us his support when everybody else thought we were mad.

And it is for:
Wendy, my travel-companion on this crazy journey and the love of my life.

CONTENTS

ACKNOWLEDGMENTS

Thanks to:
John Willis; cover painting
Tony Orvis; sketches

Black and white photographs by David Prothero

Everything in this story actually happened, although some of the stories are an amalgamation of several different occurrences.

Most of the names are the true names of the people involved, although where I was not able to contact certain people to obtain permission I have changed their names.

Available from Amazon.com and other retail outlets

Available on Kindle and other devices

Unwelcome

"Get that disgusting creature away from me, I hate dogs".

It was a beautiful sunny afternoon in May and Wendy and I were pulling up some weeds in the garden. Our new bed and breakfast had only been open for a couple of weeks and there was certainly still plenty of gardening to be done. Oscar, our wonderfully friendly, though admittedly very large Chocolate Labrador had been snoozing on the lawn. His hearing is obviously sharper than ours because by the time we realized that our new guest was walking up the path he had already jumped up excitedly and raced towards her like Scooby-Doo on speed. A consequence of spoiling Oscar (and we certainly do) is that he cannot believe that any human being would not fall instantly in love with him. In fact most people do, but this particular lady was a disgruntled and vocal exception. I grabbed his collar and to his total dismay dragged him back towards the house leaving Wendy to apologize and try to welcome our guest. We do actually keep Oscar away from people until we know whether or not they are likely to want to see him. However we state clearly on our booking confirmation that check-in time is from 4.30p.m. We will always accommodate people who wish to arrive earlier but ask them to let us know if this is the case. We had heard nothing and so were caught a little unprepared when she had arrived at 2.30. Wendy sensed that this was not the time to point out this slight difference in timing, and when I hurriedly returned from caging the dog she was politely trying to enthuse about the lovely weather and enquiring as to whether Mrs Coetzee had enjoyed her journey to Sarlat. The visitor totally ignored my wife but managed to re-find her voice as soon as I got within a couple of meters. Almost throwing the car keys at me she announced that "the luggage is in the boot, make sure you get ALL of it!" Of course I always like to carry the luggage in for our guests, but at this point we still hadn't managed to get as far as "Hello".

There were three large suitcases so I took some time to get each one upstairs, but by the time I finished Wendy seemed to have cracked the ice if not broken it, and I was surprised to receive a slightly curt "Thank-you". I have more difficulty in feigning enthusiasm than Wends, (the only person I know whose abbreviated name is exactly the same size as her actual name). So I decided the best ploy would be to get out of the way.

We met up in the kitchen a few minutes later. There were a few moments of shocked silence and I could tell that the Missus was wondering whether I might lose my temper. I'm generally a mild mannered sort of a chap, so this is an occurrence witnessed rarely but which can be a thing of great power and ferocity once released. We looked at each other, I smirked, we giggled, and then burst into fits of laughter.

Apparently Mrs C was going to unpack, make herself a

cup of tea (despite Wendy's offer to make one for her) and then come downstairs to collect a map of the town and get directions for the short walk to the medieval centre. She was to be joined by her friend from London in the early evening and at that point would require recommendations for a restaurant for dinner. So when she came stomping down the stairs five minutes later I was disarmed by a new outburst. "There are going to be three of us in the room and there are only two sets of towels. It's not very good is it? Get your people to fix it. NOW!" I scurried into the kitchen calling "My people, My people". Of course the sum total of the people who work in our chambres d'hotes is me, myself and I, plus Wendy. I didn't (and still don't to this day) know who our guests are going to be. Wends does that bit. She explained to me that the two friends were going to be joined in two days time by the daughter of the one who so far had not arrived. This obviously explained the urgency of the third set of towels.

If we'd have had a couple of successful seasons behind us I would, at this point have been asking if one of the more impersonal corporate hotels in the town might not have matched Madame's requirements more closely. But in our third week in business I found myself with a fixed smile glued firmly to my face climbing the stairs for the fourth time in fifteen minutes, carrying a set of towels which would not be used for over 48 hours. I came down again to find my wife in floods of tears. "I think we have made a terrible mistake. I can't do this."

There are two remarkable codicils to this account of the stay of our unwelcome guest. The first is that in all of our years running Le Jardin Sarlat we have never had another unwelcome guest. The second is that on leaving us Madame Coetzee thanked us profusely for our hospitality, swearing that if she ever again holidayed in France ours would be the first establishment which she would contact.

Needless to say our booking software now has a firewall second to none. And let me apologize in advance. If you enquire about availability and your surname contains a C, an O. three Es, a T and a Z, a light will flash in our office. A siren will sound. Our house will be full for the next ten years. And if you ever dare to walk through our front gate and venture up the path towards our front door you will be eaten alive by a vicious Chocolate Labrador called Oscar. Even after 4.30pm.

2

Discovery

We LOVE Italy! Well to be honest we haven't seen all of it, but the parts that we have seen were enough to make us want to live there. One of the places that we first worked together was in Rome. Wendy had an event management business rewarding high performing sales people with 5 star experiences in, amongst other places, The Eternal City.

Meanwhile I was an everyday general photographer. Fifty weddings a year feigning excitement every time someone had their "special day". Product shots for the brochures of clients who would try to explain their enthusiasm for the difference between 20 different sizes of nuts and bolts. I had a portrait studio. God knows how many babies needed "snapping". Fortunately I made some money from this because the mothers often needed 3 or 4 prints to send to the fathers. Frankly, most of the time that was because they were not sure who the father was. And I had a Kodak mini-lab processing and printing holiday snaps for people who once a year spent a week in Bennidorm.

I had aspirations to become a great landscape photographer. You may not believe me but this is a true art, because the ability to recognize the transient light which turns a pretty scene into a picture of incomparable beauty and then to interpret that light on film is as difficult as it was for Turner to replicate the scene in watercolour. I almost managed to attain the required level of skill and commitment needed to become a true photographic artist, but couldn't quite work out how to make any money out of it. So basically I was sacrificing my art to make a few quid.

Then I was asked to photograph a Christmas party for the local Building Society and, ever happy to earn cash for socializing with pretty girls, I jumped at the opportunity. Wendy had not wanted to go but had been persuaded by a friend that it would do her no harm to do a little networking. That night she won a contract to organize a series of events around Europe, beginning in Rome.

We had been friends for many years and had played together for the same squash team since we were in our early twenties. We were soccer fans and because I had worked in the sports trade we watched Everton together whenever I could get free tickets. I thought at the time that it was because we idolized Graeme Sharpe, Peter Reid and Trevor Steven. Later I worked out that it was because Wendy was in lust with Gary Lineker. I drank in a local pub because she helped out behind the bar and I realized too late that about ten other men were doing the same thing. (Actually there were about six of us but when Wends read the first draft of this book she suggested that I could exaggerate a little for the sake of her street cred). Anything for an easy life, so there were fifteen of us. We played bar games, darts, dominos, told jokes and sang songs. They were some of the most fun filled nights of my life.

Almost 5 years later we literally bumped into each other at the afore mentioned Christmas party. Wendy found a photographer, I found a job in Rome and we each found our soul-mate. The Rome event was the first of many which convinced us that we should work together, be together and love each other for the rest of our lives.

So when we got the chance we spent all of our spare time back in Italy. In Rome of course, where Wends took me to the Cavalieri Hilton and I showed her the Borghesi Palace. Where we agreed that the Bernini statue of Daphne and Apollo was the most beautiful piece of art that we had ever seen. Or to Tuscany where we marveled in Florence but stayed in St Gimignano where we explored and photographed the stunning landscape and got engaged. Where I managed to read a poem of proposal despite a pathetic bout of nervousness which almost ruined our meal, and the most threatening of thunderstorms that we had ever seen. Where Wendy ignored the portents and eventually, with a little prompting, said "yes". She married me six months later in a castle in the Yorkshire Dales.

Although we adored Italy our next door neighbor always went on holiday to France. We knew Paris well and had both spent time on the Cote d'Azure but didn't know the area that our friend loved.

"So what attracts you to the Dordogne?"

"It's like the Cotswolds, but with fantastic weather."

We are very fond of the Cotswolds and after doing a little research on the internet we quickly came to understand what he meant. The houses were constructed of the same picturesque yellow stone and the landscape appeared to roll gently and supported a great wealth of agriculture. The only obvious difference we could make out was that Bourton-on-the-Water and Stowe-on-the-Wold are divided by pretty little streams whereas La Roque Gageac and Castelnaud La Chapelle are separated by a river so wide that for centuries the only way to get from one to the other was by ferry.

At the time there where several budget airlines flying from airports across the UK into Europe. A series of television documentaries were making easy air-time by criticizing these companies because they charged extra for heavy baggage, charged 4 Euros for a coffee and didn't even allocate reserved seats. The most vilified of all the airlines was an Irish company called RyanAir which seemed to be run like a dictatorship by its CEO Michael O'Leary. We decided to check out the Dordogne and booked return flights with them between Liverpool and Bergerac. At a cost of 18 pounds sterling for the two of us we received an efficient service transporting us from the North of England to the South of France for less than the price of a 20 mile taxi journey in England. It's just over an hour in the air so you have a coffee before you go on board and don't need another. You don't reserve seats on a bus and you don't need to here either. Even if you need to pay to check extra suitcases on board (we never did) it's still cheaper than any other airline. Thank–you Mr O'Leary. (Now there's a phrase you don't hear often).

For our first mini break we stayed in Sarlat-La-Caneda. We couldn't have made a better choice.

We are admittedly country bumpkins and we were initially surprised by the size of the town. The guide books show pictures of a small mediaeval square and the expectation on arrival is that this will be the entire settlement. So driving into Sarlat, a city of 10,000 residents, we were at first a little shocked to pass shopping malls and industrial estates. There were residential apartment blocks and a college. Then car dealerships and supermarkets. Neither of us wanted to admit it to the other but it looked very much like one of the West Yorkshire towns that we had left behind. We got lost three times trying to find our accommodation and when we eventually did arrive at the B&B that I had trawled the internet to select, we were barely on speaking terms.

Then we opened a door into a 15th century courtyard with wisteria clinging to the walls. We were shown to our room which was furnished with antiques, be-draped by tapestries and which presented views of flying buttresses which supported the knave of a church which had obviously seen days of great importance. I started to believe that I had not made a mistake after all. We took a shower, had a glass of wine in the courtyard and decided to walk into the town for dinner. The sun was setting behind the tower of a smaller church to our right and it drew us into a cobbled square which seemed to become larger the closer we approached. The sky was turning orange now, silhouetting a building with a pointed spire which could only have been dreamed of by the Brothers Grimm. "Rapunzel, Rapunzel, let down your golden hair". We walked on and to our left were the largest doors I had ever seen in my life. We later discovered that the church had been restored in the late 20th century and the doors which terminated the ancient aisle had won the architect prizes for the conversion of the Eglise into an indoor market. My first thought, and one which we relayed to countless children subsequently, was that this must be the giant's house. As the sun set the square started to fill with hungry tourists. Buskers played guitar, violin or piano-accordion. Jesters teased passers bye and a human statue of Charlie Chaplin sprang to life when a small child threw a Euro into his hat. I'd seen it all before. And then dusk imperceptibly turned to dark and gradually the street lamps started to flicker. One by one the lights caught, grew in strength and took hold until the whole scene was illuminated by gas-light. Honestly, it was so beautiful that I could have cried.

The next day we slept in, enjoyed a wonderful breakfast and set off to explore the Dordogne. A brief tour of some of "Les Plus Beaux Villages de France". The "Most Beautiful Villages of France" is an official classification of, currently, 153 tourist magnets in the number one most popular tourist country in the world. Astoundingly 18 of them are within a 50km radius of Sarlat. Paris has wonderful art galleries and Monte Carlo has millionaire yachts but neither can compete with the shear natural beauty of the Dordogne. Our first stop was La Roque-Gageac. Pre-war French President Poincare wrote that La Roque-Gageac was "surely the most beautiful village in France". I for one would not disagree. Nestled at the foot of towering cliffs and hemmed in by the Dordogne river, it's picturesque setting belies a difficult past. On 17 January 1957 part of the cliff gave way and demolished some of the houses below. Three people were killed and the main road was closed for over 2 years. In 2010 there were fears of a similar disaster as water pressure built in the rocks. Turning adversity into opportunity a major engineering project was undertaken. The rocks were drained and tied and large metal nets were constructed to protect the village from further rock falls. The road was widened and a footpath was created along the river bank. The whole area was landscaped and seating areas were created among the flower beds and newly planted trees. They did a superb job and I swear that the village is even more beautiful now than it was on the day that we fell in love with it 10 years ago. However on that particular day a cocktail party was taking place at the chateau overlooking the village and elegantly dressed women were drinking Champagne whilst men in morning suits were throwing the empty bottles into the swimming pool below. Wendy has always known her place in the world and without hesitation turned to me and said "I want it Davey, buy it for me!" Meanwhile, back on planet earth….

Our next point of call was Domme, a "bastide" village

which dates back to the early days of the Knights Templar and was the sight of Philip the Bold's royal mint. It changed hands between the French and the English several times during the 100 years war, and later between the Catholics and Protestants during the wars of religion. Today it is popular for its picturesque narrow roads, two beautiful little squares and some nice bars and restaurants. There is a limestone cave and quite an arty little market on Thursday. It's most remarkable feature is that, thanks to it's elevated position, it offers perhaps the most spectacular panoramic view across the Dordogne valley. It was early November and we sat in the central square in shorts and tee shirts eating a goats cheese and pear salad with honey dressing and a glass of rose wine. Followed by a beer in the mediaeval centre of Sarlat. We had only just arrived and already we didn't want to go home.

However all good things must.. , and so back at work we started to plan our next mini break. And three months later the next.

Our third trip to Sarlat coincided with the summer solstice. Mid summers day is a huge music festival in France, and I LOVE music. I have tried to play instruments from time to time and although no-one could fault my enthusiasm I have found to my eternal regret and dismay that I possess no talent beyond a voice with perfect pitch, though no great tonality, and a catholic appreciation of those who can attain that which I would happily give an arm and a leg to accomplish. Well not a leg, but perhaps an arm. Being right handed, a left arm, obviously. From the wrist down, but preferably retaining a few fingers. Under general anaesthetic. In fact I am one of those people who has realised that they will never fulfil their ambition and so feel quite within their rights to judge the people who can. Namely "a critic". Sometimes you can appreciate others with great talent even if you do not possess that talent yourself. Nowhere is this more true for me than when I find myself in awe of musicians. This particular night in Sarlat I swear I was in heaven. We moved from one street corner where a brass band played (more saxophone than I was used to) to another where four kids were thrashing out punk songs. A string quartet tried hard to be heard above a covers band playing Floyd, Clapton and Queen. "Sarlat Country Dance" were line dancing and best of all an Irish group were playing songs by The Corrs and Thin Lizzie. We followed the bands until starvation forced us into one of the many restaurants in the main square. I ate hastily, anxious to return to the free concert. There was a new band on the main stage by now, playing first Beatles and Stones, then Stevie Wonder and Marvin Gaye. Dozens of people were "Dancing in the Street" (a cover of the Bowie and Jagger version) and by now we had consumed enough beer and wine to join them. With each new song the square seemed to get busier until there was barely enough room to dance, so we decided to sit down and catch our breath. Spotting one empty table we headed to sit down but as we approached I could hardly believe my eyes. As a photographer I immediately recognized the Canon EOS1D camera which was the only item on the table. I owned one of these myself and knew the value was in excess of 2000 pounds. I wouldn't have let mine out of my sight for a minute, so we looked around to see if we could work out who had left it. No-one seemed to be showing any interest as we sat down, ordered a drink and waited to see what would happen. After about ten minutes a young man who had been dancing in front of the stage with a group of about a dozen friends walked over, apologized that his camera had been taking up space on our table, picked it up and left with his friends. We were incredulous. In England that camera would have been gone in 30 seconds but here it had never crossed his mind that someone would steal it. I glanced up at the town hall clock and, surprised yet again, asked Wendy what time she thought it was. "Probably past midnight by now." It was 2 o'clock in the morning. There were families of grandparents, their children and their children's children happily wandering the streets. We hadn't seen a single drunken person amongst the five thousand who were out that night and we hadn't seen a single policeman. Again we compared the scene to an average Friday or Saturday night in England. Actually, to our memories of a Friday or Saturday night in England, because we were so disenchanted by the drunks and hooligans rampaging through the streets of our home market town whilst scores of police just stood and watched, that we no longer went out at the week-end. We were dressed as we would for the middle of a summers day at home but it was the middle of the night. The gas lights were illuminating the busy but still incredibly picturesque town. And then a complete stranger who had heard us speaking English came towards us with a half full bottle of white wine and addressed us in our language, rather than in hers. "Excuse me; we are leaving now, would you like to finish this?" We gratefully accepted, drank the remaining contents whilst listening to a young girl singing Elton John and Billy Joel songs, then walked back to our B&B hand in hand under a clear starlit sky. We knew then that we wanted to live in Sarlat.

3

Disenchantment.

It's surprising when we meet up with people from the UK, just how disenchanted with the country so many of them seem to be. It's all quite difficult for us to listen to because we love so much about the UK. The scenery where we lived in Yorkshire is simply magnificent. I lived in the Lake District for a few years and there it is even more spectacular. We loved to walk the dog through the Dales and call for a pub lunch. To come out of the cold into a cozy snug and sit in front of a coal fire with a pint of Timothy Taylors Landlord India Pale Ale is the most wonderful way to spend a Sunday lunch-time I can imagine. The food in England is on a par with anywhere in the world and indeed represents just about everywhere in the world. Whether you want to eat Mexican, Chinese, Thai or Italian you are never far away from an excellent restaurant serving it up. And that's before you get me started on Indian food. Actually most of the Indian restaurants around us in Yorkshire are run by families from Bangladesh, but they produce dishes of incomparable flavour from all over the continent. Our favourite curry of all time is a Murgh Hydrabadi from the Aagrah chain of restaurants which were our usual Saturday night haunts for many years.

We are self-confessed sports addicts and as such are spoiled by coming from the U.K. Although these days we tend to watch rather than compete the sheer variety of sport available is astonishing. The premier league is the most entertaining soccer competition on the planet and is watched around the world. We have truly great golf courses and Wendy and I get hysterical when Europe beat America in the Ryder cup. The only thing better is when England beat Australia in the cricket Ashes. O.K. I know that doesn't happen as often but it does make you proud when it does. We even have a tennis player now, even if Murray is a Scot when he loses and Andy is a Brit when he wins. Formula 1 seems to consist of cars which are made in Britain beating the few which are not. In the London Olympics G.B. seemed to be winning everything. We were suddenly enthusiastic about horse riding, diving, dinghy sailing and cycling events which we previously didn't know existed. The whole event was such a showcase to the rest of the world that even people who had been sceptical were swept up in a wave of patriotism bordering on jingoism.

The standard of coverage of sport on television in the U.K. is remarkable. But then the standard of British television as a whole is astonishing. The whole world watches British comedy like Fawlty Towers, dramas such as Downton Abbey or documentaries by David Attenborough. Although much maligned the BBC is a national treasure and achieves a standard and diversity of programming which cannot be matched in any other country. As a Corporation it may seem to strive for excellence rather than pecuniary advantage but, hey, let's celebrate when the artists manage to defeat the accountants once in a while.

I could go on and on about why I am proud to be British. So I will. Films like The King's Speech and The Imitation Game. Music like The Beatles, Genesis and Judie Tzuke. Universities like Oxford and Cambridge. A monarchy admired the world over and a parliamentary system copied on every continent. And, yes, a National Health Service which delivers care, free at the point of delivery, to all, rich or poor regardless of religion, gender or skin colour.

Yet we decided to leave England and emigrate to France. We were both finding it harder and harder to make a living. After 15 years running my photography business I was finding it harder and harder to find new work. The digital revolution was in full swing and people were taking more photographs than ever but they were not having them printed. They stored them on iphones, ipads or even "in the cloud", whatever the hell that is. The upshot was that everybody suddenly became a photographer and the skills I had developed over 30 years became undervalued. The one hour mini-lab industry disappeared almost overnight and took the likes of Kodak and my little shop with it. Virtually every aspect of the photographic industry changed completely in a couple of years. Meanwhile Wendy was also finding business more difficult to come by. Her clients were financial services companies and in the wake of a series of scandals they were scaling back on large events. It wasn't that they could not afford to take sales people on reward and recognition events (aka holidays), but they could no longer be seen to be doing it. Other industries still held conferences and sales events but so many "event management companies" were setting up that finding clients was increasingly cut-throat. Doing events sounds very glamorous and indeed it can be, but Wendy certainly had the best years of doing it. There are now even university courses teaching hundreds of youngsters to be event planners. At the end of their 3 year courses I suspect that about 5 per cent of them will find jobs. So we were both working harder, seeing less and less of each other and making less money. Somebody was trying to tell us something and we can take a hint. We needed a new challenge and now there was nothing to stop us from making a complete break. We don't have children and what family we do have lived some distance away from us and we certainly didn't live in each other's pockets. Wendy's parents died when she was quite young (my poor little Orphan Annie). My folks lived in Shropshire where my father had bought a smallholding in order to breed his beloved Arabian horses. We saw Mum and Dad at week-ends when we could, but getting them to come to see us was not very easy. Dad could not be prized away from the animals, so when we sadly lost him to cancer it removed the last tie that we had to England. My Mum, brother and his family and Wendy's sister and her family could all come out to see us in France. The decision was made and we set about selling everything we owned.

4

Planning

The house was easy to sell and we moved into rented accommodation to make it easier to move at short notice. Our next most valuable asset was the boat that we had moored on the river Ouse. When I was at school Mum and Dad bought a 25 foot motor boat on Lake Windermere in the Lake District and some of my happiest memories as a child were the week-ends we spent on board. Wendy and I lived in a little village called Littlethorpe which had a marina on the Ripon Canal. We longed to own a boat and almost bought one when we were doing an event near Bray on the Thames. It was very expensive and in the end we got cold feet. Then one day we were walking the dog along the canal and a 32ft Princess sailed serenely past. I was explaining to Wendy that it was the same make as Mum and Dad's boat but with a little more room in the cabin and a larger deck for sun bathing at the back. Only as it had gone past did I notice the "For Sale" sign taped to the folded down hood. We hurriedly took the dog back home and ran to catch up with the boat. You can't go too fast on the canal. It was a lot of money and with our work commitments and doubts about the Yorkshire weather we would have been crazy to buy it. So we did. We didn't get as much use out of her as we had imagined and she cost a lot to maintain and moor, but you can't measure everything in monetary terms and we had some great days out on "Kalima" with friends.

The last quality time we spent with my father before he got very ill was a gloriously sunny day sailing through Boroughbridge and towards York with Mum and Dad teasing Wendy as she battled with the heavy lock gates. I think I would have paid all the money the boat had cost just to have that day. But we couldn't take her to France so she had to go. The economy was in a poor state and luxuries like boats were not selling easily. So when we received an offer we bit the bullet and accepted, even though it was for a lot less money than we had paid.

Wendy's soft-top car also had to go. My large, but ageing estate car would be a good work horse for our new business in France so we kept that. Much to Wendy's annoyance I refused to part with the 1966 MGB sports car that I had owned for nearly twenty years. "There's more chance of me being left behind than that bloody thing" She doesn't understand classic cars.

The next thing to think about was Oscar. About ten years ago we were walking in the lake district when a couple walked towards us with a cute little chocolate labrador puppy. He was a real character, pulling on his lead, jumping in the air when we approached to pet him and yelping with excitement as we made a big fuss of him. We'd been thinking of getting a dog as Wendy had just set up her event management business and was spending most days "home alone". Once we met the puppy the decision was made. Wendy had previously had spaniels and I had golden retrievers, so we wanted a different breed and a chocky seemed to fit the bill perfectly.

One of Wendy's traits is that if she wants something she doesn't want it next month or next week she wants it NOW. So when we get home I make a coffee and take it to Wends in her office. By the time I get there she has already found a website called puppy planet. "There's a litter available in Glasgow". Glasgow I kid you not! So two days later we head up the M6, 200 miles to Scotland. There are five puppies in the litter, one bitch (which we didn't want) and four dogs. The largest dog has the kennel name Athos, and he is bolder and more playful than the others. First he has a fight with my shoe laces, then jumps onto my knee and has a little excited wee down my trousers. So basically he chooses us. We explain to the breeder that we are going to call him Oscar and she promises to call him that until he is ready to be collected in 3 weeks time. We collected Oscar and were warned that he would not settle straight away and may not eat for several days. He jumped into the back of the car and fell asleep. Waking four hours later when we got home, he ran into the garden to go to the toilet, ate a full bowl of food, found his blanket warm beneath the central heating boiler and went back to sleep. The fact that Wendy could spend time at home with Oscar during his first days with us worked perfectly in many ways. Of course her new business didn't make any money for several months but we ended up with the most delightful, intelligent, handsome (takes after his Dad) and loving dog either of us has ever had.

Now we had to make sure we could take him to France. The process is actually simpler than we had feared. He had to be inoculated against rabies and then tested a few weeks later. Once the test proved negative we had to wait for 6 months and he was tested again. Once that again proved satisfactory he was awarded his doggy passport. Wendy wanted to know if he had to have his picture in the passport. "No it's not necessary as he has been identity chipped."

"Yes but can he have a picture?"

Needless to say he now has a passport picture which proves just how handsome he is. Which is not fair as mine makes me look like a sex offender.

However all the planning was now in place. All we had to do was find our house in France.

5

Frustration.

Once we had decided to move to France it became difficult to think of anything else. Our days were filled with a mixture of excited dreams, careful planning and frantic property searching. I'm sure we must have gone to work, made the dinner, met our friends, walked Oscar and watched television but I have no recollection of any of this. I suppose that once you make the decision to move to France you are already there because anything that happened to us in England seemed to have little or no importance. We went to Living France exhibitions in Harrogate and poured for hours over French property magazines. The houses seemed so cheap compared to England that we suspected there must be a catch. On the one hand I began to believe that we could buy a house, renovate it and still be mortgage free. On the other hand every TV program we watched or story we read seemed to be a litany of DIY disasters, missed deadlines, dishonest trades people and exploded budgets. The only way to tell for sure was to get out there and see for ourselves. What quickly became apparent was that prices in Sarlat were higher than in the surrounding areas, so although it was our initial first choice location we decided to broaden our search. We started to draw up shortlists of houses across an array of prices, locations and sizes, then contacted agents to try to get more details and addresses. Unfortunately that is not the way French estate agents work. Houses can be for sale through several agents at the same time and they are, understandably, keen to make sure that they are the ones to get the commission on any sale. So they play their cards pretty close to their chest. The only way to get anywhere is to find an agent with 3 or 4 houses in a similar area and then make an appointment to see all of them. Excitedly we made three rendez-vous with agents for our next long week-end and counted the days.

If I'm honest the first appointment was a bit of a DIS-appointment. The shop window hadn't been cleaned for weeks. It would have been impossible to read the cards or view the properties displayed pinned by drawing pins to a piece of hardboard. Although as it happened the dirty window was a purely academic distraction as the photographs were so old and faded that we wouldn't have been able to make out any detail if the glass had been polished to the standard of a TV commercial for Mr Sparkle. We went in anyway, to be told that Cedric had not yet arrived. We forced a smile and agreed to wait. After about 10 minutes a funny looking tramp came into the shop. Despite the heat of the day he wore a long sheepskin coat which looked as though it had not been off his back for years, and baggy corduroy pants which were too long in the leg but which at least had the redeeming feature of covering most of his scratched and unpolished shoes. Smiling to reveal a missing front tooth he shook Wendy's hand and said "Good-morning I'm Cedric". By the time we reached his car it would be fair to say that our expectations were somewhat on the wane so we were not totally surprised when he got into a Peugeot of a model which I hadn't seen for 20 years. One door was a completely different colour to the rest of the car and when he closed it the window fell down into the cavity of the door. Fortunately (or by design) there was no interior trim on the door so Cedric was able to squeeze his hand under the glass and lift it approximately back into place where it wedged in its allocated aperture. Surprisingly the car started within about four attempts and pulled into the Sarlat traffic. Then the window fell down again. This time Cedric shrugged and left it where it was.

Admittedly the first house we saw was the least expensive of all the possibilities we had short listed but as we had advised Cedric that we were looking for a house to run as a bed and breakfast I was somewhat surprised that we had not been warned about its complete unsuitability for such a purpose. It was situated between a filling station and a workshop of indeterminate purpose but such disorder that Steptoe and Son would have tidied it up. Wendy wouldn't even get out of the car.

The second house was definitely better. The little Peugeot had surprisingly managed a 20 minute climb into the hills along narrower and narrower roads when we entered a small croft of five or six houses. Two of them were very picturesque and we were delighted to be told that the first of these was the one which was for sale. Although it was a little small we started to think of ways we could re-arrange the layout to include a kitchen and dining area. There was a downstairs bedroom which could possibly have made a living room for us, but that would have meant that we would have had to sleep in one of the upstairs bedrooms leaving only two letting rooms. We asked to see upstairs and Cedric opened a loft hatch and pulled down a ladder. We were starting to realize why houses in France were cheaper than their equivalents in England.

However things were improving and we had high hopes that our agent had saved the best 'til last. I asked about the location of the third property we were due to view. It was in the lovely village of Carsac, just ten minutes from Sarlat and our hopes were raised again. Until Cedric suggested that we view a different house further into the countryside. It seemed there was no point in viewing the third property on our list as it had been sold the previous Spring. We decided not to bother as we were already in a pretty remote area. We love the countryside but any further into the hills and no-one would ever find us. We retreated to a bar in Sarlat and sat in the sunshine with a pichet of Bergerac Rose as compensation for a frustrating day.

We had arranged to meet Claire the next morning in La Roque-Gageac and although we were 10 minutes early she was there to greet us. She was English, had lived in France for 5 years and was dressed like an estate agent. I spent 20 years in sales and know that the most important start to the sales process is to listen to what your prospective customer wants. Claire insisted on buying us a coffee and we sipped it whilst her pleasant chat about us, about herself, about the weather, imperceptibly turned to questions about the house we wanted. Why did we want to live in France, where would we prefer to be, old house or new, how many bedrooms would we need? I realized we were being quite skillfully "qualified" but after the previous day's experience that was exactly what we wanted.

The first house Claire took us to (in a large four-wheel drive) was made of ginger-bread and was being sold by Goldilocks. The shutters framed the tiny windows in a lovely shade of green, the steeply sloping stone roof was trisected by 2 elaborately carved dormer windows and mature trees stood behind it. The only thing which could have made the house look more like an illustration from a fairy-tale would have been a wisp of smoke coming from the chimney, but as the morning was already reaching 30 degrees this wasn't really necessary. Facing it was a derelict barn and I immediately understood Claire's idea. At some point your head has to over-rule your heart. I have always wanted to build a house and the total renovation the barn would have required to convert it into four en-suite bedrooms would have been the closest I had ever come to doing it. In 10 minutes I had decided how best to lay out the new rooms. However the project would have taken months if not years and we would have no income whilst we built. The price was reasonable but would have left us with very little money left to carry out the build. We both loved the cottage and could see the potential of the business we would end up with but despite Claire's insistence on buying us a lovely bottle of St Emillion at lunch (whilst she sipped water) we started to envisage more and more difficulties as we ate. By the time the cheese arrived we had essentially ruled out the possibility of buying the house and barn.

Unfortunately when you see exactly what you are looking for and then realize that you can't have it other alternatives don't seem as attractive. We saw three more houses before returning to England but nothing seemed to be perfect and we arrived back in Yorkshire a little disappointed but even more determined to fulfill our goal of a move to France. However two more unfruitful house searching trips later we concluded that we would never be able to afford the perfect house in Sarlat and decided to start looking in other areas.

6

Serendipity

It is often said that women make more words per day than men and they have to use them all up. This is certainly true of Wendy and me. I once came home from work and we decided to walk the dog. Of course I am interested in how my wife's day has been, so I let her start to tell me about it. Personally I would précis the events of the day, but Wends seems to need to give every detail, whether it contributes to the outcome of the story or not. The early evening sun was shining and Oscar was enjoying his walk even more than I was so we kept going a little further than our usual wander around the block. By the time we reached the canal we had covered about two miles. Wendy was at first puzzled why I had started to giggle, and then it dawned on her. "I've been talking a lot haven't I?" In twenty minutes I literally hadn't managed to get a word in edgeways. She seems to be able to take her breaths in the middle of a sentence so you never know when to butt in.

So when I took her phone call one busy Tuesday morning I was hoping for a brief chat. No chance. "I've found it, you should see it. It's beautiful, five letting rooms and a separate apartment for us, we'd just have to repaint the shutters because they are bright turquoise but that's only superficial, all the main restoration has been done. All the bedrooms have en-suite shower rooms except ours and that has a great big roll top bath, and the dining room has French doors overlooking the lawn and the garden is just beautiful. I can't believe it's under our budget and it has four acres of land so I can have a donkey and…"

"WHAT?"

"Well I've always wanted a donkey. Actually we'll need two so it doesn't get lonely. What shall we call them?"

"NO!"

"We can talk about that later but you've got to see this house Davey it's gorgeous".

She only calls me Davey when she wants something.

I'd had my hopes dashed already so I tried not to get too excited and stay calm but I have to admit I found it difficult to get through the day at work and drove home too quickly at the end of the afternoon. Wendy already had the details of the house she had found on the internet and we went through them together. It seemed to be exactly what we were looking for. English people looking for houses in France always get excited when land is included with a property as it is so rare and expensive in the UK. In France there is so much land available that it tends to be quite reasonably priced. What people forget is that it takes a great deal of work but I had to admit that the house surrounded by a large garden and fields looked both impressive and picturesque. I wasn't about to back down on the issue of donkeys but on the other hand it would mean that I would need a ride-on mower, so of course we had to buy this house. Unusually the house was being marketed by the vendor not an agent and there was even a UK phone number, so Wendy rang and spoke to the owner. The place had been a holiday home but the lady's son had got into a good but expensive private school so the indulgence had to go. There was some urgency, hence the very tempting price. We went through a long list of questions and virtually all the answers we got back encouraged us to think that the house was perfect for us. This was meant to be and within a couple of days we had arranged to meet the owner in France the following week.

We decided to take Mum so that she could see we were not planning to emigrate to the other side of the world, and booked a few days in Sarlat before our rendez-vous at our new home an hour further North. Then we booked a hotel in the Limousin to give us time to see a notaire and finalize the purchase. So we spent two days showing Mum the Dordogne that we had come to love and on the third morning rushed breakfast and bundled everything into the little hire car. I was just setting off when Wendy's mobile phone rang. It was Margaret, the owner of our new house, asking whether we had set off. Wendy assured her that we would be with her in about an hour and then fell uncharacteristically silent. Margaret had spent the last 3 days tidying the house and garden and then, the previous evening, had dinner with all of her French friends in the village. She had never stopped loving the house but from England it was easy to be rational about whether she really needed it. Saying good-bye to her friends for the last time she realized her son's education would have to be paid for another way. Now she was in tears on the phone to Wendy. "Please don't come, I'm so sorry but I can't bear to sell it".

To say we were devastated would be an understatement. We couldn't blame Margaret for changing her mind but once again our plans were in ruins. We had sold nearly everything we owned in England and now were envisaging yet more months in rented accommodation.

I was determined that we should try to enjoy the day. We decided not to go up to The Limousin but instead went for a ride along the Dordogne river. We went out for lunch then came back to Sarlat and to the B&B who fortunately could put us up for one more night. We went for a drink in the medieval square to enjoy the sunshine and after half an hour we started to walk back to get changed for dinner. We passed an Estate Agents window and despite saying we were going to forget about houses for a day I couldn't resist. "I don't know why you're looking in there" protested Wendy. "you know that we can't afford anything in Sarlat, you've looked a hundred times".

At that moment the greatest piece of good fortune that either of us has experienced unfolded to change the course of a day that we will never forget for the rest of our lives. Michael Edwards heard Wendy's English voice and decided to walk up to us. "Are you looking for a house in Sarlat? I'm just about to go in there to put mine on the market." Ten seconds either way and we would have missed him and almost certainly the rest of our lives would have been completely different. There is a film I love called Sliding Doors about just catching or just missing a train and how your whole life story is written according to which scenario actually takes place. I genuinely believe that in life you make your own luck, but for this life altering moment I have only serendipity to thank.

I asked Michael how much money he wanted for his house. It could have been a two bedroom cottage which would never have provided us with an income. Or it could have been a million Euro chateau which we could never have afforded. He promised that it was a four bedroom house, all en-suite, for only slightly more than our maximum budget. Ideally I would have liked five bedrooms but it seemed worth a look. Mum was tired so we sat her down with a gin and tonic in the square and walked the five minutes away from the town centre. Michael explained that the house had been empty for 2 years and warned us to expect some minor cosmetic work. He wasn't kidding. Looking back at pictures we took at the time we can see now that we were viewing it through rose tinted glasses. It was obvious even then that there was a huge amount of work to be done even to make it habitable but sometimes you just get a feeling. We walked through the front gate of "Le Jardin" and up four steps to a tree lined footpath and could not believe that we were so close to the town centre and yet the only sound we could hear was the singing of the birds. We're country bumpkins really and I don't think we could cope with a town centre but as we walked along the path towards the house we felt as though we could have been back in our beloved Yorkshire. I say walked along the path but actually we were following Michael who had produced a pair of secateurs and was cutting and hacking his way through brambles and ivy like Indiana Jones in a hurry. O.K. I could accept that this was cosmetic and although to our left there seemed to be nothing but dense undergrowth I looked to our right and could see an irregularly shaped lawn interspersed with what must once have been flower beds and two rows of beautiful apple trees. Wendy has always dreamed of having a front porch with a swing seat (she loves American movies) and by the time we got to the front door she was already imagining herself sitting on the covered terrace with a glass of wine looking down the garden. Her imagination was very accurate, we do that most days now, but I was trying to stop her showing too much enthusiasm. I was going to have to make a bid for the house if we were going to buy it and I was looking for reasons to reduce the price. I needn't have worried. Inside there were plenty of opportunities for me to point out everything that was wrong. There was damp on the walls and the whole place looked as though it had last been decorated in 1964. There was no privacy between what would become the guest's side of the house and our accommodation. The kitchen was unbearably old fashioned and the floor boards in the living room visibly sank when anyone trod on them. The three bedrooms upstairs were also a disappointment.

One was a reasonable size but furnished and decorated with total disregard for taste and maximum focus on the budget. The other two rooms were totally unsuitable. There was a sink in the corner of each and a tiny shower room and toilet. There was no room to walk round the beds let alone unpack a suitcase. A horrible disgusting smell pervaded the whole house. In fact there was very little of it we could have realistically kept. It was completely unsuitable for the way we wanted to run our business and everything was filthy dirty. And we fell hook, line and sinker in love with it.

We told Michael we had some hard thinking to do and asked if we could return the next morning. We said goodbye wearing our best pondering expressions and set off to find Mum. As soon as we were sure we were out of earshot we both started to gabble excitedly. We had both had the same ideas for the house and now we simultaneously and excitedly went through our plans.

"The space in the loft is huge; we could easily put two extra bedrooms up there."

"And convert the two tiny bedrooms into one large one. That would give us our four letting rooms."

"And take the glass door to our sitting room out of the hall and put one in the breakfast room."

"Yes, then we would be completely separate."

"And build a breakfast terrace outside the guest's sitting room for eating outside on warm days."

By the time we joined Mum for a beer we had completely redesigned the whole house. Slowly coming back to earth our thoughts turned to how much it would cost to do all the work and how long it would take to do it. We would have no income until everything was completed. By the time I had finished licking my finger and sticking it in the air (the most reasonable method I could think of to make my guestimations) there was a considerable gap between the money we had and the price Michael was asking for the house plus all the work needed. We needed a strategy.

The following morning we took Mum to see Michael and the house. She was quite brilliant, pointing out everything that was wrong, tutting and shaking her head whilst Wendy suggested ways we could solve each problem and I pointed out how much each solution would cost. Michael started to sense that we were getting a little disenchanted and started to back pedal somewhat. "If you buy the house you will save me the estate agent's fees and to be honest I could do with selling the place quickly as I have a project in England that I'm trying to finish. I'd be interested in any sensible offer." At this point I told him what we were prepared to pay and after a pretty feeble attempt to raise the price which I straight batted away Michael reached out and shook my hand.

We explained that we were going up to the Limousin for a couple of days and that we couldn't do anything until we got back to England. Michael was unperturbed. "As far as I'm concerned the house is yours unless you tell me otherwise". He suggested that we may want to come back to measure and plan things and handed us a key. After we left I thanked Mum for her excellent acting whilst pointing out all the potential problems. "What acting? I meant every word."

Bloody Hell we had bought a house in France.

On the drive up to the Limousin it started to rain. Then downpour. It didn't stop for two days. As we got closer to the hotel which we had booked in the same village as Margaret's house the few settlements seemed to get smaller and smaller. Then the settlements started to disappear altogether with only an occasional farmhouse eerily materializing through the sheeting rain. And cows. Dozens of them, no hundreds, thousands of cows. We were the only people staying at the hotel for those two nights and we realized why Margaret's house was so cheap. There were virtually no people living here and certainly no tourists, so for us no chance of a business. We could not have bought the house we had initially come to see.

The hotel served delicious Champagne though.

7

Completion

Two weeks later and we're back in France armed with a tape measure, note pad, pen and Farrow and Ball paint catalogue. There are two things all ex-pats in France agree on; you can't get good bacon and French paint is expensive rubbish. We'll miss the bacon but we can bring paint with us. We're going to need gallons. Wendy has great appreciation of colour so we decide that she should choose the schemes for the new house. The one proviso is that I can veto any decisions she makes, but as we move from room to room deciding how we are going to replace the vivid orange and purple with String, Cord and Bone we are in complete agreement. By the end of the first morning we have the measurements of every room and notes on the colours and work needed before we can open for business.

The biggest job is going to be the creation of the two new rooms in the loft space. Most French houses have bedrooms in the eaves but ours had a cavernous void and the most important reason for this visit was to find an architect. I always wanted to be an architect when I was a kid but baulked at the seven years of extra school and college. Now, however I could re-design the layout for the new place and intended to spend the next week or so doing just that. I then needed someone to draw it up properly and submit it for planning permission. In France the Mayor decides who can build what and where so the decision is usually based on whether the build will increase the Taxe d'Habitation paid to the council rather than whether it will upset anyone else. However, Le Jardin is officially within the Medieval Centre of Sarlat and part of a United Nations World Heritage Site so we have to be a bit more careful about what we do. We also decide we need an electrician as hardly any lights or sockets seem to be working. There is a local English language newspaper and through it we manage to arrange an appointment with Jerome, an architectural technician who can do the work we need far cheaper than a fully qualified architect. He simply points out that if I design it and something doesn't work it will be my responsibility not his. No pressure there then! There were several "sparkys" listed, but only Peter advertised the fact that he spoke English. At this point our French was not great so we needed a little reassurance. A phone call established that he indeed was English but had lived in the Dordogne for ten years. He was incredibly busy and didn't know when, or even whether he could do our work but he would "try to finish early tomorrow and come for a look." We implored him to do so as we were leaving the next morning and sure enough at seven in the evening a flustered Peter knocked on the front door. Thank goodness, because of all the people we have met since buying the house he has been the most helpful and useful contact. We know him now as a mild mannered and kind hearted friend. He works non-stop whilst on a job and won't pause even for a coffee let alone a bite to eat so by the time he got to us that evening he probably hadn't had anything since breakfast and because we didn't know any better we found him a little brusque. There was little conversation beyond a brief introduction and he started to scurry round the house following trails of cables as they weaved through walls and across ceilings, tutting and shaking his head in disbelief every time he got back to the fuse box. Oh-oh here we go! After about ten minutes he just started to laugh. "This lot hasn't worked in years. Half of it is fifty-year-old French wiring which was superseded twenty years ago and is probably illegal now, the other half is a DIY attempt at English wiring which fortunately stopped working at all before it set fire to anything. That half is definitely illegal. It all needs to come out and you need a complete re-wire."

We were determined to stay on budget and on time and we had failed within two days of starting work. We used to stare incredulously when naïve couples appeared on the TV design programs and insisted that they intended to build a five-bedroom mansion in three months for two thousand pounds. Were we doing the same thing? For the first time we were having doubts as we returned to England and waited each morning for the postman to deliver Peter's estimate. When the breakdown of all the electrical work needed just for us to get insurance arrived three days later we assumed that there may be other problems we hadn't thought about and added a contingency to the amount Peter said he would charge. We had not yet completed the purchase so could still get out of it and I did briefly think of doing so. Our hearts were set on living in Sarlat, though, so we decided to get tough. Michael had assured us that the house had been recently re-wired and that much other work had been done. If we were to continue with the purchase and have all this work carried out, he would have to foot the bill. We played good cop bad cop as Wendy rang him pretending to be really upset because I wanted to cancel the purchase unless he agreed to deduct the sum we needed from the price. He rang me back and offered to meet us half way so I slammed the phone down. Half an hour later he rang Wendy and agreed the new purchase price.

By the time we met Michael two months later in the July we were hardly on speaking terms but we had to complete the transaction. In France both parties to a house sale normally use the same solicitor or "Notaire" and we had agreed to use a guy named Bernard in nearby Belves. The notaires record the sale, amend the deeds and make sure all tax due has been paid. In our case the amount we were paying for the house was less than we had originally declared and this was like a red rag to a bull to the official. Convinced that we must have made a cash payment to Michael in order to reduce the official price and pay less tax Bernard virtually interrogated us for ten minutes. Fortunately, all three of us were singing from the same hymn sheet (much easier when you are actually telling the truth) and he reluctantly agreed to proceed. Which he did but not before threatening us with confiscation of the house, imprisonment in the Bastille, and possible Guillotine if he ever found out we had fiddled him. We initialed about a hundred sheets of paper, signed about twenty more and wrote him a cheque. Then Bernard turned into everyone's favourite uncle and, smiling from ear to ear, took us all for a beer in the bar across the street.

The whole process seemed to have a conciliatory effect and Michael offered to take us to his favourite restaurant in Sarlat for lunch. We followed him to a lousy snack bar which we had never used before and will certainly never use again, but as he was paying we couldn't complain. He ordered the plat du jour of a course pate of the livers of indeterminate animals followed by burned goose gizzards in a fat reduction and then a powdered milk brulee. Three courses for nine euros, yummy! We decided to play it safe by ordering a cheese omelette each and a plate of chips. The omelettes were still frozen but the chips were o.k. The conversation was polite and consisted principally of Michael expressing astonishment at our intention to charge any more than thirty euros per night for bed and breakfast. "You could stay in a real hotel for that". He finished his gruel, swilled it down with the last of his beer, wished us well, shook our hands and walked out leaving us with the bill. Oh well I'll afford him that small victory.

8

Exodus

We completed the purchase of Le Jardin in July and got planning permission to convert the loft into two bedrooms almost as soon as we returned home to Yorkshire. We were careful to design in the Perigordian style with dormer windows so we were not expecting any real problems, but we were surprised how quickly the permission came through. Now it was finally sinking in that we were going to be living in France. We had to tie up all the loose ends. Two businesses to officially close down and lots of friends to say goodbye to. We knew that it was quite possible we wouldn't see some of them again. Some people emigrate and then divide their time between England and France but we were determined not to do this. We would be busy with our new enterprise so wouldn't have time to travel for most of the year but also we wanted to make a clean break. France was to be our new home and it would be easier to settle if we accepted this and didn't try to keep one foot in each camp.

It's always a huge job to move house but this was going to be even bigger. It seemed to take weeks to pack things away into boxes. We tried to be organised as everything would have to be unpacked at the other end and it was also vital not to pack anything we would need before we left. We couldn't believe how much stuff two people could accumulate. Even so we were reluctant to get rid of things. Le Jardin was huge compared to our little cottage and we didn't want to be buying things in France that we had thrown out in England. Clothes, kitchen equipment, t.v. towels, table lamps, hundreds of C.D.s all took up lots of space but at least they all went into boxes so we could see how much room we would need in the removal lorry. However other things were not as simple. In addition to all our furniture we had bought some pieces which we had envisaged would look good in the B&B and some of them (beds, wardrobes, chests of drawers) were very bulky. Then all the gardening equipment like the lawn mower would also have to be transported along with several large shrubs and plants. We were starting to wonder whether two lorries would be enough. Finally, we thought we had worked out how much room we would need and found adverts in "Living France" magazine for companies who specialise in transporting emigrating families' worldly goods. Our plan was to get quotes for a large lorry with trailer and go with the cheapest. Except that when we got the quotes back none of them were cheap. We were guessing three or four thousand pounds but the most reasonable came in at double that and every penny we spent on getting to France was a centime we couldn't spend renovating the house. I was grumpy for three days but I knew we would just have to pay up. Our best friends Richard and Judith rang to see how we were progressing and I complained to Richard about the price the removal firms were charging and he started thinking outside the box. "Why don't we hire a couple of vans. You can drive one and we'll drive the other. It will be great fun. We will be able to stop at some auberges for meals on the way down and we can buy some booze at Calais on the way back." His enthusiasm knows no bounds when it comes to an adventure and he loves France. I didn't want to dampen his spirit or sound ungrateful for the offer but there were practical reasons why his idea wouldn't work. We needed a heavy goods vehicle and trailer not two vans and neither of us have an HGV licence and I had got to get the cars down there as well. "That's o.k. we'll make two trips". I don't think he had thought about how far it is from Yorkshire to the Dordogne but the excited schoolboy in him would not be dissuaded. "Well work out how much it would cost to do it that way. We'd love to do it wouldn't we Judith?" I could imagine Judith rolling her eyes and shaking her head. She's the practical one.

In my own mind I had all but dismissed the idea but the next morning I thought I should carry out the exercise. How long would it take? We'd need the vans long enough to load and unload twice on top of the travelling time. How much to rent the vans? I was surprised how big the vans we were licensed to drive actually were and I started to wonder whether we could fit everything into three vanloads rather than four. That would mean I could drive my old Peugeot estate car towing my little M.G. and actually save one trip. So, how much for the ferry crossings? How much diesel would we use? How much for hotels and meals at Richard's beloved auberges? By the time we had done all of that we would be physically exhausted and if it meant driving four times round Paris on the "peripherique" we would quite possibly murder each other at some point. But to my astonishment even if we paid for all of Richard and Judith's food, board and lodgings we could save nearly five thousand pounds. I checked it twice and kept getting the same answer. Having convinced myself that Richard's idea could work I was a little fearful that he and Judith would have cold feet and decide to pull out, but I should have known them better. We had a cunning plan.

We spent a couple of weeks unpacking the boxes that we had spent months filling and then repacking them looking for every cubic centimeter of saved space. We got firmer about not taking things that were not absolutely necessary and several trips to the tip in Ripon got rid of anything superfluous. Every shoe was filled with socks and ornaments were wrapped in clothes rather than the bubble wrap we had planned. Finally, we were pretty sure we could get everything into 3 vanloads and one estate-carload. Then Wendy reminded me that Oscar would be in the back of the car and we needed another rethink. "Yes, but we will be towing the M.G. and that will be empty. If we pack it from the foot wells to the rear bulkhead I bet that we could get lots of stuff in". Wendy was not convinced so we had a trial run. For a brief second I did think about putting Oscar in the M.G. but I doubt that I could have suggested that to Wendy and lived. Then I thought about taking the roof down and stacking vertically but as we would be traveling in November that wasn't my best idea either. Eventually we worked out that if we filled the M.G. with the smallest objects we could actually fit quite a lot in and that the bigger objects would be better in the vans. Then I got an inspired idea "We just have to buy a roof rack for the Peugeot". We wouldn't be leaving for another couple of weeks but we couldn't face unloading the M.G. again so everything stayed put. The Peugeot got a new roof rack.

Richard and Judith came over to Yorkshire from their home in Cheshire on the 27th of October for our leaving party. Wendy was an event planner and we never had quiet nights with a few friends around. This time obviously the party would have a French theme. There were tricolour flags and Bleu, Blanc et Rouge everywhere. Our neighbours and friends arrived in the obligatory striped jumpers, berets, strings of onions and resplendent moustaches. And that was just the women. Most of the men came as Yvette, Maria or Michelle from Allo Allo. "Listen very carefully, I will say this only once". We ate French Onion Soup and Coq au Vin and drank French wine and Cognac. We listened to La Marseillaise, Edith Piaf, Charles Aznavour and Serge Gainsbourg. I apologise to all our French friends but I can't take Johnny Hallyday seriously. We had our gunpowder plot firework display early as November 5th was to be our first night in our new home and the French don't do bonfire night. Then we drank and danced until the early hours surrounded by cardboard boxes. The next week was going to be probably the most exhausting of our lives with hours of non-stop driving and unpredictable sleep patterns, so what better way to start it than with a late night followed by a slight hangover.

Fortunately, we could have a bit of a lie in the next morning. Richard and I went to collect the two big "Luton" vans that we had ordered whilst the girls cleared up from the party. This is not as male-chauvinist as it sounds as most of our things were already packed so clearing up consisted mainly of throwing out paper cups, plates and decorations, and getting all the empty bottles and cans together. The first job for one of the vans was to get rid of all the rubbish. I did that whilst Wendy took Oscar to the kennels. Happily, the weather was kind to us and we started loading the vans at the beginning of a cold but sunny afternoon. All the hours of preparation and planning paid off and we got the majority of the furniture and boxes into the back of the two cavernous spaces with hardly any air between any of it. Wendy and Judith carried like pack horses and Rickie and I loaded and stacked everything like a giant game of Jenga. It would be even more like Jenga when we had to take everything out. We drank coffee 'til it came out of our ears and finished in time for a take-away pizza dinner and an early night on inflatable camp-beds.

The alarm was set for 6.30 but Wendy and I were too excited to sleep properly and were wide awake by 5am. Luckily (for us not them) Richard and Judith were too uncomfortable to sleep well and we were almost ready to leave before the alarms went off. Richard is officially the comic strip super-hero "Gadgetman" and rummaging into his miraculous utility belt he produced a couple of walkie-talkies. They would be useful if we wanted to chat or lost each other or needed to pull in for a pit-stop. We had to get them working and then learn how to operate them properly. Just to check the range Richard walked down the hill into the village and back. Now satisfied that they would be fine he just had to set the satellite navigation app to guide us to Portsmouth and we left just before lunch. Breaker one niner, looks like we got us a convoy. Let's put the hammer down but watch out for the smokey bears. You got a suicide jockey on your donkey. Affirmative, good buddy. We had exhausted all the cb radio jokes by the time we got to the end of the M6 so we switched them off to save the batteries. Ace on the Bass and Cruisin for a Bruisin turned off onto the M5. Back Alley Sally and Shady Lady had a little nap.

We arrived in Portsmouth just after dark. After a slight altercation with a jobsworth at the docks who wanted to charge us extra because we were a commercial enterprise we went across the road and had a bar snack in a great little pub. With the vans safely loaded onto the night-ferry we settled down for the night. I had booked a cabin for four in order to save money. Remember when you were a kid and went to a friends house for a sleep-over. You couldn't think of anything to say all day but as soon as the lights went out you couldn't stop talking. I think I got to sleep at about 4am and at 5.30 the tannoy announced the reveille and ordered us to our vehicles.

The drive from Caen through France was nothing short of magical. We stuck to the almost deserted little roads between sleepy towns with names like Verneuil-Le-Chateau and Savigny-Sous-Fais. A slight mist hovered above meandering rivers and shafts of sunlight dodged between the shadows of the plane trees which lined our route. We stopped in a hamlet which seemed to consist of three houses, a town hall and a gambling bar. All French villages have a town hall and a gambling bar it's just the number of houses that varies. The bar was full of disheveled men who eyed us suspiciously and silently listened as we ordered coffee and croissants. Satisfied that we were not aliens from another planet or plain clothes gendarmes they returned to their card game and drank Pastis. They ordered more drinks before we left at 8.30.

As lunch time approached we found ourselves in a lovely little town with two restaurants. The first had an elegant waiter, white table-cloths, a menu starting at fifty euros and no customers. The second was just what we were looking for. Dozens of white vans were parked outside so we added two more to the total and walked into a lovely lawned garden where about thirty men were tucking into a plat-du-jour and drinking red wine. A pleasant young man offered us an aperitif, turned and walked off to fetch two small beers and two glasses of white wine. Richard, upset that he had not taken our food order, followed him into the kitchen. Richard has little French but total confidence in his ability to communicate and we could see him waving his arms, peeping into pans and pointing at a menu. The astonished chef burst out laughing, took off his apron, threw it at Richard and went outside for a cigarette. A minute later and Richard emerged from the kitchen with a pretty little waitress. Between them they carried four plates of shepherd's pie and were followed by an excited collie dog. The pie smelled (and tasted) delicious so the dog sized up the situation, worked out the best chance of receiving tit-bits and sat on Wendy's feet. The whole thing was tremendous.

By late afternoon our enthusiasm for the narrow roads and little villages was wearing thin. We kept getting stuck behind tractors that seemed oblivious to the fact that we were there. I think farmers on tractors should be banned from roads. We don't drive our cars on their fields do we? Getting irritable, we decided to look for the more direct route. Even the Motorway was quiet and we were soon making good time. Even so it was getting dark by the time we came to the sign for Sarlat. We had a conference on the walkie-talkies because the signs said one way and the sat-nav said another. Aware that signposts often disappear half way along a route I decided to trust TomTom. A big mistake as the little roads got windier and narrower as we approached Sarlat. We've looked for the route we took that night for years and we just can't find it. Finally, arriving grumpy and exhausted, we left the vans outside Le

Jardin and walked into town to the B&B I had booked for two nights. A little snack and a good long sleep in cozy comfortable beds.

The following morning we awoke to clear skies and a slight frost. In fact it was the kind of late autumn day that we have come to treasure in the Dordogne. OK it can get cold but it's lovely in the sunshine and as long as you wear layers it's perfect for walking the dog or tidying up in the garden. However, on this day Oscar was still in the kennels in Yorkshire and our new garden was a very long way down our list of priorities. So after a leisurely breakfast we walked to Le Jardin to begin the task of unloading the vans. One slight problem with our new house is that there is no direct access by car, so everything had to be carried up the cobbled path 60 yards to the front door. Fortunately Wends had labeled all the boxes so we knew which ones contained things which we would need straight away. The girls opened these whilst Richard and I lugged yet more boxes to the house. The boxes we didn't need were just piled up in what was to become the guest's sitting-room. Wendy and I could unpack these later. The morning was a bit repetitious but not too tiring and after a light snack for lunch we still had the time and energy for a lovely walk and a beer in the medieval centre before a nice dinner and another good night's sleep.

9

Home

The alarm clock woke me and for a brief moment I wished that I had not set the annoying little gadget for so early. Then I remembered that the next leg of our "adventure" lay ahead. It was to be probably the longest drive we would have and a prompt start would be essential, so I sprang excitedly from the bed to open the curtains. Oh. Snow! Shit!! We had been assured that it hardly ever snows in Sarlat and to be fair it hardly ever does. However the timing this particular day could have been better and my excitement was already turning to concern. It was time for a board meeting and we woke Richard and Judith to discuss a course of action. Of course I had overlooked the fact that Richard had been a keen member of a rally team and the news of the latest meteorological challenge sent my ever ebullient friend into raptures. " The vans will be great in the snow, we'll just take it easy and we'll be at the motorway in no time" It was at this point that I remembered being told that the French don't grit or salt the roads in winter and that our TomTom had a propensity to seek out the most obscure roads in France. Far from being back in England the next day I now had visions of two white vans up to their roofs in snow and their frozen contents being discovered by a French farmer several days later. "Don't the mad English know to stay in bed all day if it snows?" Actually the French don't even need snow as an excuse and habitually stay in bed all day if it gets a bit chilly. I'm sure that they have got it right but Richard is bigger than me and can be very persuasive so by ten o'clock the four of us were slip sliding away through the forest. Richard was on a special rally stage, frequently pulling ahead of me and then having to wait until I caught up. I was tip-toeing around every corner and praying to any God who would listen that Julie the sat-nav knew where she was going. Wendy was gripping the door handles as if she might decide that jumping out was her preferred option at any moment. As far as I could tell Judith was having a little nap. Then as we came out of the forest it stopped snowing. By mid-day the sun came out and the snow started to turn to slushy water. As we pulled onto the motorway the day looked every bit as beautiful as the previous day had been. Lewis Hamilton the Formula 1 champion has an expression "Hammer Time". I'm not sure exactly what that means but it's something along the lines of "now it's time to drive very fast". I thought that was the whole point of Formula 1 but for now we had a ferry to catch and lost time to regain. The poor vans roared and shook as we ignored the speed limits on the almost empty roads and raced North. I'm sure that was Niko Rosberg we just overtook.

We made the ferry on time and dozed fitfully before the long trudge back up to Yorkshire, finally arriving in wind and driving rain. Fortunately the bad weather cleared overnight in time for us to load up our wagon-train ready for the last leg of our journey. One of the vans had to be returned to the hire company and the other was filled to the rafters (if vans have rafters) with the rest of our worldly belongings. It was mostly things from the garden. Lawn-mowers, rakes and spades, pot plants, a glass-fibre pond and two beautiful small trees which we had bought so recently that we were determined not to leave behind. Everything was the wrong shape to fit the available space and we had at least three attempts at cramming everything in. Every suggestion that we should just leave something behind to save space caused an argument. "If there's enough room for your golf clubs you can find space for my bird table". Fortunately just as the atmosphere was getting a little tense Judith had a recollection of the opening sequence of a TV program we had all loved decades earlier. The Beverly Hilbillies had struck oil and, just like us, were moving house. "So they loaded up the truck and they moved to Beverly" We could all remember the scene as the family's pick-up truck was weighed down with old farm equipment as they re-located to the city of swimming pools. It got funnier still as we realised that we had a solution to our space problem. Judith would have to travel as Granny Clampett had done, roped to a rocking chair on the roof of the van.

Wendy and I started to load my old Peugeot and the MG. We let Richard finish the van on his own. Eventually everything was aboard except for three new duvets which we had bought the week before at Ikea. We could easily have bought them in France but it just goes to show how we doubted that anything familiar would be available when we "moved abroad". We had already overcome bigger obstacles than this and I simply popped the bonnet on the MG and packed the plastic bag covered bedding around the engine. Finally chaining the front wishbones of my beloved classic car to an A Frame and attaching that to the Peugeot's tow-bar, I delegated the last job of the day to my wife. The cork popped loudly and effervescent Champagne filled four flutes. The toast was to dear friends and to Yorkshire, the beautiful county that the four of us had called home for most of our lives. Richard and Judith were now settled in Cheshire and the next day Wendy and I would be immigrating to France.

The plan was to take the Euro-tunnel train as Wendy would not leave Oscar alone in the back of the car on the ferry. She can be very claustrophobic and I was not sure how she would react to being 250 feet beneath the English Channel in a 30 miles long tube but she was adamant that this was our only option. However as we approached the port Wends was getting more and more agitated. The claustrophobia may have been a contributory factor but it manifested itself as worry about the dog. Oscar, of course was his usual relaxed self. He has always loved the car and except for his occasional excursions to stand up, turn round, lie down again and sigh before going back to sleep, we wouldn't have known that he was there. He had passed the tests following his inoculations and we had all the necessary paperwork. We had booked him onto the train and we had a sticker of a dog's paw on the windscreen to signify that we had an animal in the car. Yet Wendy was not happy. She kept opening the envelope which held his papers, re-reading them and checking that everything was present and correct. "What if they won't let him go?"

"Why on earth would they not let him go, we've done everything we're required to do" I reasoned. But one can't reason with Wendy when she is worried about any animal let alone our beloved chocky. "I'm not going if they won't let him cross".

"Well I'm going so you'll have a long walk back".

"You wouldn't say that if you loved him"

Actually I shouldn't have said that because I love both of them but fortunately we were approaching the customs point so the argument died down as we prepared our three passports and documentation.

A green neon sign flashed "Welcome Mr and Mrs Prothero" as we approached the barrier. The clever number-plate recognition trick impressed me way beyond any logical response and I turned to Wendy "At least we're in the correct car".

"It didn't say anything about Oscar though" and the argument kicked off again. Then we noticed that the customs officer was on his radio and his colleagues were all heading towards us. For the first time I started to get nervous and I wound down the window to ask if everything was O.K. Then I realized that they were all laughing at us.

"We've just never seen an MG Roadster used as a removal wagon before" he giggled. "Can I see your passports please?" After a cursory glance he handed back our documents. "I see you've got a dog with you". Wendy went into full panic mode and how the customs guy didn't immediately assume we were smuggling cocaine I'll never know. She thrust Oscar's documentation at the unsuspecting officer and blurted. "He's in the back, do you want me to get him out of the car? He's had all his rabies jabs. Look, this is his passport." But the official was peering into the back of the estate car and smiling with affection at Oscar. "He's asleep. Don't bother getting him out it's a shame to wake him. Have a nice journey". Our little family was heading for France.

We were going to be driving down through the Loire valley and I was really looking forward to it. It is a part of France that we really didn't know and a couple of people had told me that it is just as beautiful as the Dordogne. I know I'm biased but honestly it isn't. The landscape is flatter so what natural beauty there is can't really be appreciated from the roads. However I do have to concede that the famous chateaux along the valley are magnificent. They are much younger than the chateaux that we have in Aquitaine and of course they are more like palaces than castles. They are proudly ostentatious and seeing them eerily reminds one why the French Revolution took place. We stayed overnight at a hotel in the grounds of Chateau Chaumont. Once the scene of some of the most extravagant parties ever held in France it looks like the archetypal aristocratic trophy of unimaginable wealth. Today's equivalent would be the Playboy Mansion or Trump Towers and I found it impressive, though a little vulgar. To a starving French peasant it must have seemed vile. The hotel was pleasant enough, if starting to look like it needed a refurb. We took Oscar for a little walk around the gardens and settled into the rooms. We've stayed in a few hotels in France where the decor has not been to our taste and this was certainly one of them. You couldn't say there was anything wrong with it but purple and orange walls with net curtains over the windows would not be the way we would decorate a bedroom. So we left Oscar to enjoy (or not) the handy-work of The Stevie Wonder Interior Design Company and joined Richard and Judith in the splendid dining room. Richard and I had two of the worst beers ever and sent them back, deciding to stick to wine. The meal was expensive and dreadful, the service over-formal and unfriendly and the wine was average and extortionate. Feeling a little cheated Richard and I ordered a single malt scotch and sipped it in the lounge whilst the ladies, and everyone else went to bed. In an effort to finally obtain a little value for money we stole a brochure from the honesty rack at reception and called it a night. If this is representative of French hotels no wonder they are complaining that Bed and Breakfasts are stealing all their trade. I went to bed still hungry but quite encouraged and optimistic.

We woke to a glorious blue sky and the sun throwing shafts of light through the last remaining golden leaves into the bedroom. I was tempted to un-hitch the MG and go for a drive through the country lanes around the village, but the little car was acting as a skip and I had nowhere to put everything she was carrying. Instead the five of us went for a leisurely walk through the tranquil gardens of the chateau. In the warm morning light the palace seemed more welcoming than it had been the previous day and we seemed to appreciate the architecture with more enthusiasm. The gardens were quite formal and absolutely enormous. The ever trusting Oscar ran through the fallen leaves and skipped excitedly from side to side. A couple riding two elegant white horses wished us a good day. We could easily have stayed longer but we were eager to press on towards Sarlat.

When we turned into Rue du Jardin de Madame about five hours later the whole street seemed deserted. We all parked outside our new front gate. Wendy, Oscar and I in the old Peugeot followed by the older MG and then Richard and Judith in the Transit van. We could almost sense the shutters of our new neighbour's houses creek open a little wider as they tried to decide whether the house had indeed been purchased by "the English gypsies". We all hugged each other, then I carried Wendy over the threshold and through the large front door. The house was freezing. We had four working light bulbs and six working sockets. Months of hard work lay ahead converting this sorry old building into a welcoming Inn where people from around the world would want to spend their hard earned vacations. It was the most daunting prospect we had ever experienced, but it didn't matter. We were home.

10

Beginning

We took a few days to rest and recuperate. There was no rush to get everything unpacked and frankly we were exhausted. For a couple of days we slept until mid morning, went for walks into town and sat at Les Iles bar enjoying a beer or three. Soon, though, Wendy and I were itching to get started. Three days after we arrived in Sarlat Richard and Judith set off on their final journey of the adventure and headed home. There were big hugs all round and not a few tears. The simple fact is that we could never have managed our relocation by ourselves and their help had turned what could have been a killer of a trip into an extremely fun and enjoyable week. They also saved us a fortune, which as things turned out we were to need before very long. As my old Auntie Lizzie used to say "houses have hungry mouths".

For now though Wends and I rolled our sleeves up and got to work. November can be quite wet here but for our first month we hardly saw a cloud. The days were spent in the garden. For days and days all I did was pull up ivy from the flower beds and what was left of the lawn. Wendy cut back shrubs and small trees and swept paths clear of the millions of leaves which had fallen from the larger trees. Fortunately we had a piece of land at the back of the house which came as part of the purchase and we piled dozens of wheel-barrow loads onto a compost heap which seemed to double in size each day. I discovered that my wife is a pyromaniac and she kept a bonfire going for days on end. Getting tired of my superhuman mission to rid the garden of ivy I set myself a new challenge. There were about twenty banana trees shading what was going to be the breakfast terrace. Each was at least fifteen feet tall and their dense broad leaves were preventing any light from getting to the rest of the plants beneath them. They had to go, so I set about chopping down the plants and digging up the roots which were about the length and breadth of an elephant's front leg. With a mixture of spades, a couple of axes and a crow bar I set about the huge task, whilst Oscar "helped" by following me around like an infuriating foreman. After about two hours I was getting so fed-up of having to move him every time I wanted to swing an axe that I lost my temper and shouted at him to get the hell out of my way. He's not used to being shouted at. He's so well behaved that it rarely happens, so sulkily he wandered off through the thick undergrowth of shrubs and plants like David Bellamy in the jungle. It was at this point that he discovered the first of what we now know to be three ponds in the garden. There was an almighty splash, a yelp, a scrambling sound, further splashing and finally a series of loud barks. Hurriedly I tried to dash towards the direction of the commotion but the vegetation was too high and thick. I don't know which of us was the more surprised when we eventually came face to face. I had scratched my face and arms on the

64

brambles and then banged my forehead on a low branch and was bleeding from about five places. My problems were as nothing compared to the bemused dog facing me though. Having clambered out of the pond, extricated himself from a tangle of weed and fought his way towards the frantic sound of me calling him, Oscar was soaked to the bone and covered from the points of his ears to the tips of his toes in slime. The world's first green chocolate Labrador. He stood for a moment, still in shock and trying to decide whether I was still mad at him. Then he decided the safest course of action was to run away. Which he did, brushing past me and covering my trousers with the disgusting mix of water, weeds and algae. Barking as he ran he found the comparatively open space of the lawn and ran around it's 200 metre circumference at full speed. Three times. Exhausted he fell panting to the floor and finally stopped barking. Wendy came running out from the house having heard the kafuffle and started shouting at me. When anything happens to Oscar it's always my fault so I was expecting that, but when she eventually caught site of her beloved boy staring up at us with a perplexed expression even she had to laugh. In fact we were both in hysterics until Oscar realised that perhaps a new game had begun, started barking again and jumped all over us. It took everybody hours to get cleaned up and Oscar has had a morbid hatred of the hose-pipe ever since.

As the sun went down each evening we would move inside and sort through the boxes which filled the sitting room. We had placed larger pieces of furniture away from the walls in the rooms they would eventually find a home, but despite labelling each box we still had smaller items to search for as we needed them. Wendy needed bed sheets, pillows, towels, fluffy cushions, knives and forks, and food. Of course my priorities were Hi-Fi systems, CDs, DVDs, lap tops, electric drills and pieces of art for the walls. Once we were completely exhausted we would halt work, have a wash and make our way to Avenue Gambetta. Almost every town in France has a street, hotel or bar named after the prominent 19th century statesman. Our Gambetta is the nearest street of shops, cafes, hairdressers and estate agents to Le Jardin. In time we would get to know all the workers and inhabitants of this busy little village within a town, but for now all we needed was the take-away and the gambling bar. We would order a pizza then pop over the road for a pint or two. At first it was usually just one but occasionally one of the customers in the bar would break away from the horse racing on the t.v., introduce themselves, shake my hand and kiss Wendy on each cheek. This is actually the reason they wanted to introduce themselves as few women ever ventured inside the bar, but as ever they were extremely polite. They would be intrigued by our faltering French and absolutely mystified by our lack of interest in the horse-racing (gambling is one of the few vices I never had) but they would inevitably insist on buying us a drink. Jean-Marc the owner of the bar soon realised we were good for his business and started to make a big fuss of us. J-M is a Yul Brynner look alike and at first is a bit intimidating but he's actually a jovial and endearing chap who seems to be friends with everybody in the town. After we had made a few more visits he too started to insist on buying us a drink and we would end up having to stay for three. This was great except that when we went to collect the pizzas they were stone cold. We would walk home for half an hour of watching t.v. with a pizza box on our knees. We would crash into bed, usually before ten, and then start working again the next day. Surprisingly we had few arguments and after a week or so we could get into most of the rooms without falling over things.

Which was just as well as Peter, the electrician arrived to make a start on the re-wire. As ever he was busy and couldn't begin the work properly until after Christmas but he had promised to get us a few more lights and sockets working before Christmas and was good to his word. Mum was coming over just after Christmas and she can't stand the cold. Peter left us with heat, light and power to two bedrooms, the hall, living room and kitchen, and an instruction to ring him if we had any problems. "I'm not going away so even if it's Christmas Day just call and I'll pop round. We'll do the rest of the work in January." Top Man!

Peter also told us about a family of English builders who had lived in France for ten years who could probably do the work constructing the two bedrooms we wanted on the top floor. We met them the following week and were amazed to discover that Alan and his two sons

Simon and Mathew were originally from Pickering, about 15 miles from where we had lived in Yorkshire. Not only did they speak our language but they spoke it with the correct accent. A reet good do. We couldn't believe how well things were going. Alan's estimate was very close to my "guestimate" and they could start the work in mid January. We agreed, shook hands on the spot and chatted for an hour about our mutual love for Manchester United.

I had to get started on my side of the building work, which initially meant knocking down the walls between the two first floor bedrooms we were planning to convert to one larger bedroom. I love jobs that involve hitting things with a big hammer and soon there was brick, rubble and dust everywhere. Two brick fireplace had to come out as well and as we approached Christmas all I had done was destroy things. Everything took longer because we had to get rid of all the rubble which meant getting countless heavy sacks down the garden path, into the back of the car and up to the local tip. It was exhausting work and Wendy and I awarded ourselves the nick-name "the packhorse Protheros". One blessing though was that the staff at the tip were incredibly helpful. Before we left England I had tried to get rid of a hire-van full of rubbish at the tip in Ripon. After waiting half an hour outside the stinking filthy yard before anyone would let me in I had a row with a jobsworth who wanted to charge me for tipping industrial waste. He could clearly see that all I had was household junk but because I was in a van he assumed that house clearances were my source of income. In the end I told him that I was going to fly-tip it all on the moors and offered him my address in case he wanted to report me to the police.

"This time you'd better empty it here then."

"There won't be another time, I'm going to live in France to get away from clowns like you."

People who hate their job should get another job. At the "decheterie" in Sarlat, meanwhile, we drove into an immaculately clean and tidy tarmac yard and were helped by the staff to throw our waste down a shoot into a skip a metre below our feet. If they were not too busy the attendants would even brush up after us. It probably speaks volumes about our complete and utter lack of a social life at this time but our visits to the tip soon became the highlight of our days. There is a perception amongst some English that nothing works in France. Sometimes they have a point, but just as often they should come here to learn how to do things properly. There, I feel better now that I've got that off my chest.

Stibboh

Oblib and Odorf loved to play in the woods near their home, a large oak tree in the magical Revodnew Forest in the South of England where lots of things were back to front. They chased the rabbits and squirrels and climbed the trees, laughing and joking all day long. But they each had an annoying habit. Odorf was for ever poking a finger into his ear and Oblib just wouldn't stop picking his nose. Their mother told them and told them to stop but they took no notice. In desperation their mother told them that if they didn't do as she said they would turn to stone if the wind changed direction. They thought this was a huge joke, skipping and picking and

poking as they ran off to the woods.

Then the wind changed.......

Six hundred years later they were found by a man from Marlowe on Thames. The man took them both back to his little shop and hung a sign around their necks appealing for someone to look after them. That's where Wendy saw them and decided to give them a new home. They lived in North Yorkshire for three years and then immigrated to France with us. When you stay at Le Jardin you may just find them in the garden.

11

Christmas

Every afternoon we would take time out from working on the house to walk Oscar. We found a nice circular route with not too much traffic which took us about twenty minutes to stroll around and we began to look forward to a break from knocking walls down and destroying weeds in the garden. A couple of times we had said hello to a friendly old chap who seemed to walk his little dog at about the same time as us and one day he wandered over for a chat. He spoke quickly with a strong Occitan patois (an ancient regional dialect still used extensively here, especially amongst the elderly) and we struggled to understand much of what he said. As soon as he realised that we were English his speech slowed and became considerably closer to the French we had learned in school. He already knew some English people in Sarlat, he explained. He liked them, they were very kind and polite. He also knew some Portuguese who were equally polite, although they worked too hard and made too much money. The "foreigners" whom he disliked the most however were the Parisians. He reserved a special gesture for the people of his capital city which I had not seen before. It involved holding his nose with the thumb and fore-finger of his left hand whilst wafting the open palm of his right behind his trousers and thrusting his bottom backwards. He realised that his actions had made us laugh and his face lit up with twinkling eyes and a huge smile which betrayed an almost complete absence of teeth. We learned that his name was George and that everybody called him Juju (although we never learned why) and that his little dog was a King Charles Spaniel called Bambi. He learned that we had bought Le Jardin and was delighted because "a beautiful house like that should not remain empty with no love". We would meet him regularly after this first chat and it became obvious that, whilst he liked the English, it was one particular English woman that he liked the most. His favourite tactic would be to wait until Wendy slightly mispronounced a French word and, placing his hand on her shoulder, would say the word slowly and clearly, then make her repeat it. If I mispronounced a word (which I'm sure I did on many occasions) he would just look at me with disdain. Wendy called him her *professeur* and he started to teach her French swear words. Then we started to notice that the hand he laid on her shoulder was getting gradually further towards her chest. Wends spent many years working in offices full of men and she can handle herself well if necessary, but George meant no harm and if it gave an old man a little pleasure... It was funny how much more restrained he was when, as on several occasions, he was accompanied by his wife Denise. Madame was at least twenty years his junior and kept him on a far shorter lead than either of them kept Bambi.

It was the week before Christmas and we were excitedly anticipating a quiet day together on the 25th. A lie in, scrambled eggs and smoked salmon, Champagne, a long walk with Oscar and then the full turkey dinner. In fact we were just planning it as we took Oscar on his afternoon stroll, when around the corner heading towards us came George, Denise and Bambi. After the usual polite chat they asked what we were doing for Christmas. Not expecting to be ambushed I explained that we would be spending the day by ourselves but George and Denise would have none of it. We couldn't be alone on Christmas Day, we must have Christmas dinner with their family. We spectacularly failed to think on our feet and before we knew it everything had been arranged. We were spending our first Christmas day in Sarlat with our French neighbours. Becoming a little short tempered as we carried on our walk, each of us blamed the other for not thinking of an excuse to get out of their well-meaning invitation. I suggested we could have our Christmas day on the 26th but apparently that was a bloody stupid idea. The only thing for it was to turn up as arranged and try to enjoy it.

When we knocked on their door at just after 1.00pm everyone else was already there. Denise had definitely said *après-midi* but I should have remembered that lunch in France is always at 12 noon. Oh-well, the French have a saying "better an hour late than a minute early" and no-body seemed particularly upset. It turned out that the family members were actually Denise's relatives. She has four sisters and two brothers (not unusual in Sarlat where most people are Catholic) and two thirds of them were here with the odd aunt and a couple of cousins. Juju introduced us as his wealthy

English friends from the Chateau du Jardin and everyone looked suitably impressed and deferential. If they could have seen the state of our house that day it may have been a different story. Of course none of them spoke any English and we began to anticipate a difficult few hours ahead. A couple of the men were already getting stuck into the Pastice so when Denise suggested an aperitif we were not sure what to expect, but the reassuring pop of a Champagne cork signalled a good start to the afternoon. Wendy is a little fussy about what she eats and had been dreading the meal ahead. "You do know they eat snails, frogs and horses don't you. At the very best it will probably be goose." When everyone was seated and the first course arrived she was relieved, therefore, to be given a plate of foie-gras. We should have known that the ubiquitous delicacy of the Perigord would make an appearance. Some people have a moral objection to eating it and as animal lovers we completely understand their decision, especially when terms such as "force fed" and "fatty liver" are habitually applied. In fact all the ducks and geese are free range and would force-feed themselves naturally before migrating, so they queue up for dinner each day. The terms sound worse than the reality, and anyway it's delicious. Especially when, as here, it is served with thickly sliced fresh bread, sweet onion chutney and a glass or two of its classic partner, the golden semi sweet Monbazillac wine. Next up was a huge plate of prawns in a garlic and whiskey butter. Not Mrs P's favourite but as it came on a plate to share rather than individually portioned she got away with just picking at a couple whilst she sipped at its accompanying dry Chablis. I loved them and ate Wendy's share anyway. Conversation was getting easier now. Remarkably our French was improving spectacularly with each glass of wine and we chatted for ages before the main course arrived. To our slight surprise and huge relief Denise was not carrying a horse but the largest roast chicken I had ever seen. It was just like Sunday lunch in England except that the bird was complete with feet and claws, which the French seemed to be competing to pick at, and the head and beak tucked under a wing. We helped ourselves to a couple of slices of moist breast each and poured some thin but rich gravy and a glass each of the surprisingly light Bordeaux red. At this point George asked if anybody would mind if he had the head. We thought he was joking until he snapped the bird's neck, carved through the skin and picked the skull up with his fingers. Crunching away as if he were eating a brandy-snap, he left just the beak. Noticing our stares of disbelief George suddenly turned very serious for the first time since we had met him. "You had rationing during the war didn't you?"

"Well we weren't born but our parents remembered it, yes"

"We didn't have anything to ration and when there is no food you eat everything you can get." It soon became apparent that George's life had been defined by the war in a way that people of my generation find

76

hard to fully understand. Following Petain's armistice with the Germans in June 1940 young French were forced to labour for the Nazis, who held two million French soldiers hostage in Germany to ensure the cooperation of the new French government in Vichy. In many ways Petain had no choice and he could claim to have saved France from complete occupation by maintaining at least a semblance of independence. George, however hated the traitor and saw his collaboration with the Nazis as nothing short of surrender. He launched into a tirade about famine and the reasons the French eat horsemeat. There was even a story about the Parisians breaking into the zoo and eating the elephants. I checked this story later and indeed it was true, even if it had happened some seventy years previous to the date that George had implied, during the Franco Prussian war. The war stories went on for a good quarter of an hour until the other diners started yawning pointedly and getting up from the table. Juju's jovial demeanor returned as quickly as it had left and he ended the subject with one last observation. "Mind-you, if every Frenchman who tells you he was in The Resistance had been in The Resistance the Germans would only have been here for two weeks".

Denise brought cheese with port and then cake with a sticky sweet wine. We made our excuses about needing to walk Oscar and staggered straight back home for a late afternoon sleep.

Our friend George died the following year. Our first

French funeral. Bambi, broken hearted, followed her beloved master less than a month later.

12

Renovation

After Christmas the race began in earnest. I started to put stoothing walls up in what was to become the largest bedroom. A false floor had to go into the bathroom to enable the plumbing to be moved from one side of the room to another and a shower, toilet and sink unit had to be installed. Our daily visits to the tip were replaced by daily visits to Brico Marche the local DIY store. I'm convinced that we should have shares in that place we have spent so much money there. One morning we had a particularly long list of things we needed to carry on the work so we took one of the largest shopping trollies into the store. It still gives us a laugh that the French call a trolley a "chariot" but there has to be a limit to the number of times I can call Wendy Boedicea and she can call me Ben Hur. Anyway I digress, we loaded the trolley with tiles, tiling cement, grout and a tile cutter and headed for the plumbing section. There was an announcement over the store's speaker system but it wasn't very clear and we were too busy to concentrate on translating the garbled French, so we carried on loading pipes, joints and glue. Eventually I got a tap on the shoulder and was told that we must leave the shop. "You must go now it's twelve o'clock and we have to eat". I hadn't realised the time and still hadn't really come to terms with the imperative closure of businesses just when customers need them.

In Britain we could buy things virtually 24/7, but in Sarlat even the sandwich shop closes for lunch. I'm sure we could have offered the staff at Brico 1,000 Euros overtime and they would still think having two hours lunch with their families was more important. "O.K. we'll just pay for these then we'll go"

"No, you don't understand, we are closed now it is lunch time".

"So what do we do with everything in this trolley?" The guy looked at me as though I was an imbecile or from another planet. Or probably both.

"Just leave it there and come back at 2.15". We had just been thrown out of a DIY store! I was fuming. We needed the things we had loaded up to carry on with our work and now we would just be wasting two hours. I stomped back to the car and, no doubt somewhat erratically, started to speed home. Then as the steam from my ears started to fog the windscreen Wendy got the giggles. "You know we can't come to France because we love the relaxed way of life and laid back sense of priorities and then get annoyed because not everything happens like clock-work. That is the pay-off." So I took a deep breath, smiled and slowed down. We went home for lunch and had a glass of wine. Imperceptibly I was becoming French.

The builders arrived during the third week of January and cut an access into the cavernous space beneath the roof. Ladders lead from the first floor landing and scaffolding started to climb the outside walls to the roof. Some broken tiles had to be replaced and two chimneys knocked out. In some places one could see straight through the roof and see the sky. In a couple of places a little wood-worm was evident. Fortunately there was no sign of termites, a more expensive problem altogether, but Simon insisted that we should treat all the beams. "Once you get plaster board over all these you don't want to be ripping it all out again if the beams start falling apart." Good point well made. Then we had to consider the insulation for the roof. The traditional synthetic woollen glass fibre stuff was the cheapest, but at about four inches thick it would start to impact on the headroom in the new second floor bedrooms Fortunately NASA had developed a new system which was only half an inch thick and more thermally efficient. Unfortunately it was about five times the price. After two weeks of admittedly working very hard the builders hadn't actually started building anything. Laying the new floor would be the first stage but they couldn't begin until we had made a decision about the new staircase. Simon had recommended an artisan carpenter from the same village as they lived and towards the end of the month he came to survey the job. Monsieur Marceau had the loudest voice I have ever heard. French people generally speak with a loud voice except when worshipping in church or a fine restaurant, but Monsieur Marceau bellowed with such ferocity that Oscar ran out of the house and went to lie at the bottom of the garden. "Perhaps working all day with the wood-working machines has made him deaf" I suggested to Wendy, who decided to test my theory by standing behind him and whispering "Would you like a coffee Monsieur?"

"NO THANKS I'VE HAD LUNCH" So that was the end of that theory. Perhaps it was to save money on phone calls. He only lived five miles away and I'm sure his wife would be able to hear every word he said. He started making drawings and taking measurements as we spoke. I wanted to make the new staircase as close to the beautiful existing staircase as we could but it seemed that would not be possible. For a start the old one was made of elm and it is now virtually impossible to get hold of. It would be far better to make a clear distinction between the two, building the new flight in a lighter wood but a similar style to the old one. This would tell the history of the house and be very lovely. He showed us pictures of two different styles of staircase. The first was of the kind habitually used in England. A half flight lead to a small landing where two 90 degree turns took one to the bottom of a second half flight which lead up to the second floor. Hand rails were straight and also turned at 90 degrees. The second sets of photographs were of a far more elegant construction. Similar in style to our existing stairs, each rise turned at a different angle to form a rounded horse-shoe. The rails were curved and became steeper as the stairs got straighter. Marceau obviously loved this style and, having virtually dismissed the earlier example, began to enthuse about the virtues of the second examples. Not only were they more aesthetically pleasing they were far safer. "Every step as one climbs or descends is exactly the same length and height. The banister is always at exactly the same height. You could close your eyes and safely run up and down these stairs". His excitement whilst describing the staircase could not have been just sales patter, he could not wait to start the project. I just had one concern though. I had not realised quite how much room the open staircase would take up on the floor-plan of the two bedrooms. We had thought that the two rooms on the second floor would be huge whilst looking at the open space, but with the addition of insulation, concerns about limited headroom and now a large hole in the floor we were beginning to run out of space. Monsieur thought for a moment, and then started shouting again. He spoke so quickly that I couldn't quite understand his idea. Simon though, spoke French more fluently and seemed to be listening with a mixture of bewilderment and admiration. "He says we can hang metal rods from the roof beams and attach a floating floor. It would give you an extra three square meters" he explained, sensing that I was out of my depth. "Have you tried that before?" he asked Marceau.

"Of course."

"And it works?"

"Of course."

"You're a very clever man!"

"Of course."

All we needed now was a price. Having seen standard sized flights of stairs at Brico-Marche for under three hundred Euros my guess was about five hundred. I was wrong by a factor of five, and that was for the cheaper square cornered design. The preferred curving staircase was another two thousand on top of that. The suspended floor would also be an added cost. We were back in the land of Grand Designs. Everything was more expensive than we had hoped and I was determined not to go over budget. I thought we had built in a big enough contingency but now that was running out. Wendy and I had a quick board meeting and fortunately were of one mind. We would have loved to order the better staircase but reluctantly told M. Marceau that we would have to go for the cheaper alternative. "You can't do that to this beautiful house, you will ruin it. The house is traditional and French and you want to turn it into a modern English box." We didn't want to but we felt we had no choice. Simon and Matthew agreed with the Frenchman and warned that we would certainly regret our decision in the years to come. They were all probably right but I signed an order for the less expensive solution and the three of them begrudgingly left us feeling a little bid down for the first time since we had started work on the house. The money was running out and we had no income at all. We needed another board meeting, and probably a longer one this time. So we trudged around to Jean-Mark's Bar Gambetta and bought beer. A great solution David, well done.

An hour later though and we had a plan. The two obvious things were that we needed to get the house finished quickly, and that we needed to get some bookings. I had planned to market the business through the internet but I couldn't even build a web-site without pictures and none of the rooms were ready. Our plan was to dress the rooms for a photo shoot. One bedroom only had plaster on one wall, so we put a bed against that wall and photographed it with a view of the garden through the window. One bathroom didn't have the tile floor laid so I added one in Photoshop. We also used lots of pictures of Sarlat and the picturesque villages along The Dordogne with flowery descriptions of Le Jardin. We didn't have a usable house yet but we could have a web-site.

13

Deadline

The web-site went live the first week of February and two days later we received an email enquiry for the middle of April. We didn't dare to take it though as the house was still full of trades men and builders and there was no way it would be finished in time. Two days later, though, and we had another enquiry for five days in June. The American couple were delighted that we could "squeeze them in". They paid a deposit on pay-pal and Wendy banked 100Euros. We had a business. Over the next few days we received more demands for accommodation from the USA, Australia and the UK and for the first time we were making nearly as much money as we were spending at the DIY shop. One email went unanswered for almost a whole day because Wendy thought I would do it and I thought she would. We realised that we needed to put a system in place. We shouldn't be duplicating jobs and more importantly we couldn't be missing them. I'm the creative one who flits from one thing to another and Wendy is methodical and organised, so we decided she should answer the emails and look after the diary. I would do the marketing and get people to contact us. Wendy would take over from there. So one morning I was in the kitchen having a coffee and day-dreaming about whether Manchester United would win the European cup again this year when Wendy came in from the office. "What are you up to?"

"Just planning a special offer campaign for next month. What's new?"

"We've got an enquiry for May 13th. What do you think?" There was still an awful lot of work to do but on the other hand the sooner we could open the sooner we would start earning properly. We knew from Wendy's business that there was nothing like a deadline to get things finished. Determining that we would do whatever it took to complete the work we accepted the booking and took another deposit. We had eight weeks to finish the house.

The builders couldn't believe what we had done and said it's just not going to happen. We told them it was so we'd better work out how. They had just put down the floor in the two upstairs bedrooms and Alan was just starting work on the Dormer windows. I suggested that I could put up the stud walls and plasterboard, but they didn't want to lose the work which I think they thought would see them through to probably the end of June. In the end they insisted that they could do it but not yet as Monsieur Marceau didn't want any walls in the way until he had fitted the new staircase. I couldn't see what difference it would make but then Simon dropped the bombshell. They wouldn't be here for the next ten days as they had a roof to finish and the weather forecast was favourable for them to do that. It was the closest we came to falling out but they left with no doubt that May 13th was the deadline if they wanted to get paid. I rang the carpenter and made an appointment for him to fit the staircase a couple of days later. He was already a week later than he had originally promised but arrived as arranged, at seven o'clock on the Monday morning in a battered old van with his two sons in tow. He started barking orders at the two young men who did exactly as he told them without question or hesitation. "I wonder how they know when he's cross with them" wondered Wendy, "he shouts at them all the time." Cross or not the lads carried the kit of bespoke stair parts which had been manufactured in their workshop up our garden path. Then I noticed the curved banister rails they had propped against the wall in the hall. Rushing to the first floor landing I could see that the little assembled boxes each consisted of three unequal stair treads. He had made the curved staircase. At first I was worried that my poor French had let me down but I soon remembered that I had signed the order which clearly stated the price, so I challenged Marceau. He looked at me with something approaching disdain, put his fist to his chest and in the quietest voice I had ever heard him employ said "My heart wouldn't let me, the price is the same." This was a true artisan who was not capable of making an inferior product. Many months later, once the business was up and running, we would call at his workshop and make an additional payment, but for now I was lost for words. The staircase was assembled in six hours by the three men who would not even stop for a *petit café* and it was just magnificent. We have since recommended him many times to people who are renovating properties here and he must have made a lot of money as a result. So he was not only an artisan but also a canny businessman. Please just stop bloody shouting.

Wendy and I started setting the alarm clock for very early morning. I was finishing the plumbing and Wendy was painting anything which was not moving and a few things that were as well. It was now too late for me to tackle the construction of the walls on the first floor and reluctantly I had to agree to pay the builders to do it. In fairness when they did come back on site they worked like Trojans. They arrived with two other workers who seemed to do nothing for days but carry heavy plaster boards up three flights of stairs. Peter the "sparky" was wiring lighting and sockets even as the walls were being built. Alan single-handedly completed the construction of the two dormer windows, which looked as if they had been built at the same time as the rest of the house and really added character. We found out a few weeks later that he had suffered a heart attack and I have to admit to a few pangs of guilt. Fortunately he was O.K. soon afterwards. We had met a friend of Peter's who seemed to be able to turn his hand to almost anything. His name was Julian but we called him Google because he already knew everything. We roped him in to join the effort and he did a fantastic job of tiling the bathrooms. Wendy and I tried to help as much as we could, but with so many tradesmen on site we were probably just getting in the way so we ran errands and made coffee. For a week or so the workmen arrived before 8am and left after 8pm. The transformation was remarkable but there was still much to do when Simon pulled me to one side. "We've tried David but there is just too much to do. You've got to tell Wendy to go to plan B. You need to find hotel rooms for the guests who are arriving and put them off coming." Wendy had been told similar things many times whilst running her event management business. "We can't get the delegates there on time". "The Gala Dinner is going to be an hour late". Even on one occasion, "The room is going to be closed because the prime minister is using it". Every time she would threaten, coerce or flirt with people in order to get the job done. And the job did get done. Every time. Now however she was exhausted and dejected. We didn't have only one couple coming in. We had continued to take bookings and there was a steady flow of guests due to arrive from mid May. Cancelling bookings would not just mean lost income, we would also have to refund the deposits we had taken and already spent. There was a week to go and we were running out of options. So when Judith rang from Cheshire that evening to find out how things were going she could sense straight away that Wends was struggling even to talk about it. Eventually she broke down in floods of tears and there was, temporarily, silence from her friend. Then "Do you want us to come and help?"

"Yes"

Twenty minutes later we learned that Richard and Judith were booked on the first flight from Liverpool to Bergerac the next morning. You sometimes hear boasts along the lines of "I've got 387 friends on Facebook" or similar. I'm always a bit sceptical but I know one thing with absolute certainty. Any couple with two friends as loving and kind as Judith and Richard are to us are blessed indeed!

Wendy picked them up at the airport and I went to Perigueux to buy furniture. We needed bedside tables, table lamps and even carpets. I was somewhat surprised that Wendy trusted me to go and choose them all but we know each others taste and we just couldn't afford the time to both go. They beat me back to the house and were already at work cleaning and painting. Richard was already in the process of removing the shutters from the windows and planning to rub them down and repaint them. Judith had made a list of jobs to be done (she does lists does Judith) and was prioritising them and allocating time slots to each. We unloaded the van and I assembled flat-pack furniture until midnight.

Three days later and the builders had finished fitting the last skirting boards and architrave. They shook my hand, kissed Wendy, wished us good luck and vowed to sleep for at least a week. Julian had laid the last of the bathroom tiles and was now grouting and Richard, having labelled each shutter and then painted over the labels, was trying to make each of them fit the correct windows. All he had to do now was build a breakfast terrace out of wooden decking. We started to believe that everything was going to be "alright on the night" and celebrated with a three course banquet from

McDonalds. On the day the guests were due to arrive all the construction, electrics, plumbing, tiling and painting had been completed. Richard just had to finish the breakfast terrace and I had two carpets to fit and the last few pieces of furniture to put together. The girls were vacuuming, cleaning and polishing. We were tired but confident now and the ipod was getting a good work-out. The Americans were due after 4.30 and we were close to finishing with an hour to spare. Richard completed the decking and made his way round to the front door where he was surprised to meet a jovial couple pulling suit cases. He had the wit to invite them in to the guest's sitting room. "I'm sorry I'm not sure where they are at the moment. Would you like a glass of wine? I'll go and find them". Judith carried on polishing windows whilst Wendy ran downstairs to introduce herself. "Sorry the room will be a few minutes yet, David is just making the bed." Upstairs, armed with spanners, a screw-driver and a couple of alan-keys I was doing just that: making the bed. We finally got them to their room about quarter of an hour later and they gushed about how pretty everything was. We thought we had got away with it by the skin of our teeth but at breakfast our amused guests looked at Wends and said "Be honest, we're your first guests aren't we?" The smell of paint must have given us away.

Lily

Lily lives next to our waterfall and takes care of her friends the bats, lizards, dragonflies and frogs. She is very quiet and calm during the day, but when the house goes dark at night she wakes Odorf and Oblib and Rusty, Rosie and Nutkin the red squirrels and they all have a big party.

Some people don't believe the last bit, but remember, every time someone says they don't believe in fairies a fairy dies somewhere. We would hate to lose Lily.

14

Fragility

There was not even a suggestion of a cloud and only Mr O'Leary's Ryan Air planes had the audacity to interrupt the azure sky by criss-crossing their vapour trails en route to England or Spain.

All four rooms were occupied but a family of four had made their own beds and told us not to bother vacuuming or cleaning their bathrooms. "We don't do it every day at home so why do we need it here." We gave them clean towels and emptied the bins but we had done that and serviced the other rooms by 1.0'clock and Wendy decided that gave her time to weed the garden and for me to mow the lawn, but I suddenly became brave and said "no"! We had worked virtually non-stop for 3 months since we opened and I decided that we could take the opportunity to grab some "R&R" "This is not why we came to France. Get your sun bed onto the breakfast terrace, change into a bikini and enjoy some sun. I'm going in the swimming pool"!

The business was going well. Our third guests were a couple from Australia who thanked us as they left but queried why we were not on Trip Advisor. The Travel web site had been promoted heavily on TV in Australia and U.S.A. but not as yet in the UK and we had not heard of it. The Aussies promised to give us a glowing review and were as good as their word. Two days later we got our first 5 star review followed quickly by 3 more and the email enquiries went through the roof.

The business plan I had prepared forecast that we would have 300 nights booked in the first year and by the end of May we already had 400. We had settled well and had many friends in the town, some English but many French. We had worked hard to get to the point where we were both happy and successful but now it was time for a little reward. So when Wendy joined me in the pool 20 minutes later she brought 2 glasses of Champagne. We were joined by the family of four who helped us finish the bottle (as if we needed assistance). We changed and walked into Sarlat for dinner. Even at dinner though we could not help but talk about the business and we spent an hour of self-congratulation and forward planning based on the success that Le Jardin had become. We went to bed that night a little tipsy. Well actually more than a little. I had vague recollections of Wendy doing a pole dance with the lamppost at the end of the street, and I awoke the next morning with a head still spinning from the euphoria of the night before.

I walked Oscar, went to the boulangerie and helped Wendy put out the breakfasts. Then I turned on the TV news. "A volcanic eruption in Iceland has created a huge cloud of dust which is now drifting across the UK. All flights from UK airports have been suspended indefinitely". The last word of the report hit me like a sledge hammer. The vast majority of our guests flew here from the UK or Paris. It seemed that they would now not be able to get here. No great problem if this was to be for a day or two. We live in France and air traffic controllers strikes are a regular if irritating fact of life, but this could go on for days or weeks. In months our money would be running out.

The family of four were due to drive back to England and catch the ferry home so no problem for them. The guests who were due to take their rooms were coming from Stanstead and had no chance of getting here. We had an Australian girl who had to be in Paris in 2 days' time to get home via Dubai. We had an American couple who were heading for Geneva and needed to be there for a conference within 3 days. Wendy reverted to type and got her event manager head on. Whilst our guests flapped and panicked she thought laterally about the options that might work. The Ausssie girl could catch a train from Toulouse to Nice and from there a plane to Dubai in time to catch her connection to Sydney. I just do as I am told so I drove her the 2 hours to Toulouse.

The Americans were easier to accommodate as there is a train from Perigueux to Lyon and from there to Geneva so the next day I drove them to Perigueux.

A week passed before the news brought tidings of a trial flight through the ash cloud. It seemed the only people more scared of losing money than me were the airlines. The following day the Civil Aviation Authority decided it was safe to fly after all. I awoke on the 10th morning of the emergency to another azure sky. I have never been so happy to see a vapour trail from an aeroplane in my life.

We were very fortunate. The English family of four decided that the ports were too busy to battle their way home and decided to stay 2 more nights. As the couple who were due to stay in one of the rooms couldn't get here we were able to accommodate them. So by the time the planes started to fly again we had only lost 100 euros. Then we went to service the room vacated by the American couple we had driven to Perigueux to find that they had left us 100 euros tip.

It was an exciting two weeks, but taught us an important lesson. We had been caught up in congratulating ourselves on our success, but we realised that our achievements were vulnerable to the least of events beyond our control. If you want to make God laugh tell him you have a plan.

In September Sarlat holds a patrimony night. It is when we celebrate our heritage and the people who lived here before us. Those people are represented by a candle and the Mairie give out thousands of tea lights to the houses and shops around the medieval centre. The candles line every path and window sill. One of the things the French do well must surely be a festival. It costs a fortune and we as tax payers, foot the bill, but as the spectacle is so utterly beautiful it would be churlish to moan. Wendy tells guests that it is so wonderful that the first time she saw it she cried. Actually we both cried but not just because of the incredible sight of 10,000 candles in what is an extraordinarily pretty town. No words were passed but we both knew that we were crying because we seriously doubted that Wendy would see the following year's patrimony night. She had become ill two weeks previously and just couldn't eat without being sick or having diarrhoea. She lost over 2 stones in a fortnight and trust me Wends doesn't have that much fat to lose. We never said the "C" word but you could tell that everyone she met was thinking it. Wendy was scared and I was praying to a God I don't believe in. Then the French health service kicked in. Yet another reason that we pay so much tax and again such a wonderful system that we don't begrudge paying a centime.

Wendy's GP had seen her five days previously and seemed fairly unconcerned. When he saw her the day after the patrimony night he hardly recognised her. Within 2 hours she was at the radiology lab and 2 hours after that we saw the oncologist. The French system starts by eliminating the most dangerous scenarios and by 2 o'clock in that afternoon we knew that Wendy didn't have Cancer. A meeting the following day with the gastroenterologist explored the chances that she had contracted a tropical disease. No we hadn't been to Africa. Yes it is possible that someone she had been in contact with had. Our guests come from all over the world and Wendy cleans their toilets. It's a glamorous life running a B&B.

We will never know what caused Wendy's illness, but the only thing that matters is that they found a way to control it. Within a month she was starting to eat chicken and putting on weight. She still can't eat duck or sniff foie gras without her symptoms returning but now we know how to manage them. During our first season of running Le Jardin we got stressed every time a guest broke a cup or spilled wine on a duvet. These things matter but Wendy's illness taught us an important lesson. When things go wrong now we try hard to remember that it is not vital. No matter how happy we are or how well our business is doing we have come face to face with the fragility of the human condition. Everything else is "JUST STUFF".

Tom

I have two jobs that I have to do every morning before breakfast. I walk Oscar, the choccy lab. Then I go for the bread. I know this doesn't sound particularly taxing but all Wendy does is prepare the breakfasts. And iron the sheets and make the beds. And vacuum the carpets and mop the floors. Then load the dishwasher whilst advising the guests where to go each day. Then clean the rooms and wash the bedding ready for her to do the ironing the next day. So it seems like a fair division of labour to me.

One Saturday morning on the way to the boulengerie I started to wander around the brocante stalls on Sarlat's celebrated market. A small statue of a boy standing on a wooden box caught my eye. The box had a circular hole at the front where a clock had once been, and the boy was lovingly holding a small dog. Or a medium sized cat or a very large rat. It's quite difficult to tell really. It wasn't expensive but I managed to negotiate a discount due to the absence of the clock. I named the boy Tom and carried him home and placed him in about seven places in the garden until I decided where he would like to be. Finally placing him half way down the front path where he could welcome the guests I ran in to tell Wendy of my new purchase. I was sure she would fall in love with Tom and congratulate me on my resourcefulness. She did fall in love with Tom but wasn't very happy with me. I'd forgotten to fetch the bread.

18

Sarladaises

People often ask whether the French have been friendly since we came to live here. I have to say that they couldn't have been nicer. The people of Sarlat (the Sarladaises) welcomed us with fruit, bottles of wine and pastries as soon as we moved in. We now have many French friends here and love the respect, courtesy and politeness which they show to other people.

However they can be a little eccentric. One morning on the way to the Boulangerie I had a couple of encounters which typified this.

It was a beautiful October day and the sun was already warming the air. I turned into Place Marc Busson, a small square with four lovely plane trees. The leaves were falling and formed a deep carpet on the ground. I saw a young girl skipping and kicking through the leaves as she moved away from me and I smiled at her sheer joy. Then she turned towards me and I realised that she was at least70 years old.

Laughing to myself, I turned the corner onto the main road. Ahead of me a car pulled in and a waitress from one of the bars jumped out. I was just about to shout hello when she set off at a sprint. There was an incline in the footpath ahead and she planted her left foot hard against it and performed a perfect back summersault. Landing on her right foot she carried on walking as if nothing had happened. I applauded and shouted

"Bravo". Turning in surprise that she had an audience she gave an embarrassed curtsy and walked on. We try not to analyse things like that now. It's much easier to just shrug your shoulders and say "French!"

As you walk around Sarlat you may well come across another of the town's great characters, a little chap in a policeman's cap and a luminous jacket. This is George, one of our most famous residents. Glinglin as the locals call him (an affectionate term for village idiot) has always wanted to be a policeman, but unfortunately he never quite managed to pass the entrance exam. Even so he puts in a full shift from 9 in the morning 'til 7 in the evening. He helps tourists by giving directions, but rarely to the place that they want to go. Be sure not to miss his special James Bond gadget. To you and me it looks like a pair of Binoculars, but to George it can be reversed to act as a speed camera. He used to look like a proper Gendarme but one day he jumped into the road with an arm raised to stop a car at the traffic lights. Unfortunately the lights were on green at the time. The driver braked hard and came to a sudden halt but unfortunately the Dutch driver of the car behind didn't react as quickly and realised that Glinglin was not a proper policeman just as his car ran into the one in front. Not sure whether to blame George or the other driver he made certain of getting retribution and punched them both. Now the real police insist that George wears the luminous jacket.

The most impressive piece of law enforcement we ever saw from George took place outside the Post Office. A gentleman walking his dog was being watched by our volunteer officer when the dog decided it needed to go to the toilet. George immediately marched towards the startled chap whilst scribbling in his notebook. Determinedly he tore the ticket from his pad and presented it to the dog!

It is worth Googling "Glinglin Sarlat" and watching some of his Youtube videos, he's become quite a star.

19

Fetes

Some of the "fetes" that our councilors stage every year are definitely aimed at attracting tourists. The majority of them are definitely for the locals though. The truffle festival, the foie-gras festival, the theatre festival and the film festival are either held during winter or exclusively in French. They cost a fortune but make life here a constant wonder for the full time residents. The most expensive of all must be the Christmas village. There is an ice-skating rink for the kids (and big kids) and about 40 temporary stalls selling everything from local wines and beers to handmade wooden toys. Each year there is a different theme. We have had Arabian Nights with camel rides and birds of prey, a French Canadian theme with Red Indians (sorry, Native Americans doesn't sound right to my generation) and a Magical theme with conjurors and jugglers. Our favorite, unsurprisingly, was the stall selling Champagne and chilli cheese. So as ever we complain about paying the council tax but rejoice that we live in such a wonderful town. However one year L'Essor Sarladaise, our equivalent of The Cricklewood Herald, started to complain that the Village Noel was becoming too predictable. The French use the word "spectacle" more literally than we do, so a spectacle becomes something to look at rather than something spectacular and in this case the newspaper had a good point. There is always a great atmosphere in the town before Christmas but the event was becoming a bit like a boring girl in a new frock. Something different to look at but not particularly exciting. So, stung by the criticism, the Mairie (our councillors) came up with a radical solution. Spend more money. This year there was to be a "magical and exciting" launch at 5.30 on the first Saturday of December.

We joined hundreds of excited families rendez-vous-ing as instructed in the Place de Liberte. The majority of people congregated in front of the town hall where there was a new and very pretty electric Christmas tree. However we noticed that the enormous doors of L'Eglise Sainte Marie had been illuminated by red and orange uplighters and that an area in front of them had been cordoned off, so we took a gamble that something was going to happen there. Our assumption was verified when three very important looking men ducked under the barrier and started pointing. All French men believe that theirs is the most important job in the world and that civilization as we know it would come to a halt if they did not carry it out. Give them a uniform or, in this case, a hi-viz jacket and everything becomes even more imperative. We worked out that something must be about to happen when, under the close supervision of his two colleagues, one of them gravely removed the grate which must be taken away before the door's electric motors push the mighty structures apart. Our theory was that Father Christmas was about to emerge from the deconsecrated church, probably on a reindeer drawn sled. We eagerly awaited the town clock to herald the beginning of proceedings. Cameras were trained on the doors. Windows opened on the top floor of the town hall and we began to wonder whether we had misread the situation, and then all the lights went out. It was like being on the front row of a Rolling Stones concert just before Mick runs onstage in the full glare of a SuperTrooper spotlight. Well, O.K. not that exciting, but it was pretty good stuff for Sarlat. Nothing happened for a few seconds and you could sense a slight bewilderment among the gathered citizens. Then the three council workers started running around like headless chickens. Plugs were un-plugged and re-plugged. Trailing sockets were replaced. Head torches were donned and tool boxes hastily carried into the cavernous building. Eventually a long lead appeared from the far side of the alleyway and was carefully laid right across the large doors. It would all have been very funny but December evenings get pretty cold here and the children were starting to become a little disenchanted. Then one by one the lights started to come back on. Cameras were being refocused as we realised that the cone of a spot light from the town hall's open window was moving through the star-lit sky like a Second World War searchlight. Quickly we strained our necks upwards as the bright oval of light settled some sixty feet above our heads on a window just below the apex of the church roof. And out of the window came Father Christmas's bottom. Not literally his bottom obviously, he was wearing his red coat, but he was climbing out of the window bottom first. His arms followed, then his head and then his legs and we realised that Santa was either going to commit suicide or abseil down the front of the church. The rope around his waist became apparent as, to everyone's relief it slowly started to lower Saint Nicholas towards the ground. This Saint, however was no Simon Templar. Nor for that matter was he James Bond or Ethan Hunt. In fact he looked more like an old man trying to escape a burning building. He let go of the rope for a fraction of a second to wave to the adoring children below, but had to grab the rope again as he started to fall backwards. He dangled precariously as he hurtled towards the ground at the astonishing velocity of about 3 yards per fortnight and for the next ten seconds we thought the whole extravaganza could go either way. Then the magic happened. A plume of smoke emerged from the slightly ajar doors of the church and as the sky became hazy it started to snow. Strangely all the snowflakes were emanating from the same window that had just ejected Santa but it didn't matter. The crystals were glittering as the spotlight hit them and glowing in the haze of the smoke. The children started to shout "Pere Noel Pere Noel" as Father Christmas gained his confidence and, finding a more comfortable if semi horizontal pose, began to wave with not just both hands but with both feet too. We couldn't help but laugh, but it was not in a mocking way at all. This was truly beautiful. The children were ecstatic as Santa slowly descended to the ground and into the arms of his loving wife who had obviously never expected to see him alive again.

As Santa walked into the crowd to distribute sweets to the little children older kids started to walk down the town hall steps carrying flaming torches and then from the other side of the square an elf appeared on a ten foot high bicycle accompanied by two equally tall fairies sprinkling fairy dust, and they lead everyone on a parade to the village noel.

What a fantastic event. Well done and thank-you to the Mairie.

17

Mum

It is a huge pleasure to us that my Mother, aged 82, is still able to travel and visits us probably four or five times a year. She lives close to my brother in Cheshire so martin drops her off at John Lennon airport and Wendy or I meet her at Bergerac. The drive back to Sarlat always seems to fly by as Mum recounts stories of the people she sat next to on the plane. " They have a house south of Bergerac, he's called James and her name was Janet, or Jane. Anyway it doesn't matter. Do you know them?" "They sometimes have friends come over so I gave them one of your cards. You might not hear from them but you never know. That reminds me I need to take some more cards as I always give them to my friends. They all think I am so lucky to have a son who lives in the South of France. I never tell them exactly where you are so I think they assume you are in St Tropez or Monte Carlo"

An hour later as we pull into Sarlat Mum runs out of things to tell us. "Anyway how are you both ?"

She normally spends Christmas with Martin and his family and, as they usually go skiing in January, she comes to us for New Year. Having booked a flight to get here she will often leave her first visit of the year open ended "I'll probably stay about 10 days " Watching the weather forecast on BBC she sees reports of snow and blizzards in Cheshire and decides "I might as well stop a bit" then checks Ryan Air for return flights in February. Last year she was going to come in May for a week. "It's a stupid website is that. I pressed the wrong button and now I'm coming for a fortnight"!

Fortunately Wendy and Mum get on really well and we spend hours during her visits in the car. Mum and Dad used to drive for hours through the Yorkshire Dales or later in the Welsh mountains and there is nothing she enjoys more. One morning we set off for a drive around the villages in the Lot to the West of Sarlat. After half an hour Mum was getting puzzled by the names of the villages. "It's very confusing, why do so many of them end with AC ?" I explained that villages which were loyal to the French crown during the 100 years war were granted the honour of adding the suffix AC to their name. Many chose to do so and Salign became Salignac, Beyn became Beynac. Wendy had learnt something new and concurred enthusiastically "That must be why Castelnaud, the English village doesn't end in AC"

It doesn't take much for Mum to become effusively proud of her two sons and here was an opportunity. "He's so knowledgeable, I don't know where he gets it all from. He always was good at History you know"

I can't help it, I'm just a giggler. Some people can keep a dead-pan face, but if I try to suppress a laugh my shoulders start to shake. It's involuntary. Wendy rumbled me first "You just made that up didn't you?" "Yes"

If, as a child, I had leaned forward and started clipping Mum around the head whilst she was driving I would have been given an excoriating lecture about road safety, but Octogenarians don't seem to be bound by such rules. Fortunately I managed not to crash the car as I ducked and weaved.

Incidentally even Google doesn't seem to have a definitive answer to her question. The suffix seems to be of Roman origin. One version seems to be that "AC" means "the land belonging to", so Beyn would have owned Beynac. Another explanation is that it derives from "aqua", although some of the villages do not seem to be on the river. Anyway I like my explanation best !

18

Lamborghini

Yesterday I bought a Lamborghini Miura. I owned one when I was ten years old, but as it was only about two inches long and had the words Matchbox Superfast written where the exhaust pipe should have been, it didn't really count. Then when I was about twelve years old Dad took me and a school pal to London to see the Earls Court Motor Show. The Miura on the Lamborghini stand was a shining blue masterpiece and one of the most beautiful cars I have ever seen to this day. Often Miuras were lime green or orange with bright yellow suede upholstery but this light navy example glowed under the exhibition spotlights and the cream leather interior looked as comfortable as a Scandinavian sofa. Ferrucio Lamborghini started as a tractor manufacturer but after a dispute about the poor build quality of a Ferrari he owned he resolved to make an Italian "supercar" worthy of the accolade. After a couple of false starts the Bertone designed Miura finally fulfilled his ambition. The purchase of my dark royal blue V12 dream fulfilled mine. Wendy bought a thirty metre Princess yacht in Antibes harbour, two Arabian horses and a donkey.

This morning I checked the lottery ticket and to my complete and utter astonishment we only had two of the required lucky numbers on our paper. We won three Euros but obviously I had to cancel the Lambo, the Princess yacht still belongs to the swarthy gentleman who is trying to sell her and the horses and donkey will have to wait another week before they begin their new lives in the equine paradise which is the Dordogne.

I don't usually gamble. I've never so much as joined a works syndicate to put ten pounds on the Grand National, but one day Wendy and I were sitting outside The Salamander Bar on Avenue Gambetta and noticed a poster for the Euro Lottery outside the *tabac* opposite. Whilst complaining about the obscene amount of money the winners of the jackpot could win (this day it was over 50 million Euros) we started to fantasize about what we would do if we ever got so lucky. We really enjoyed the exercise; a little bit of escapism from the hard work and endless worry about money in the early days of our business. The only problem was that we were even more unlikely to win than the stream of our neighbours who were filing into the shop and alighting clutching a packet of Gauloises and a lottery ticket. They say that your chances of winning the lottery are about the same as being struck by lightening. Twice. In the same place. But our chance was the square root of sweet nothing at all. The only way we could think of improving our odds was to actually cross the road and buy a ticket, so we did exactly that. The next morning we found the web-site of FDJ, the lottery company, to check our winnings, which of course were none existent. Even so we had enjoyed the evening at The Salamander and the following Friday evening we walked round there again, armed with our 2 Euros stake money. The weather was awful, so for the first time we went inside the bar. We had sat outside several times but had always been put off going inside. The same people always seemed to be there and although it was considerably smarter than Jean-Marc's Bar Gambetta it was obviously a local's bar. The gentlemen standing at the bar all turned to wish us a good evening and even the card school sitting at one of the tables briefly suspended activity so that the participants could say hello. We couldn't actually get a drink because the chap who had served us outside the previous week was one of the card players, but we were in no rush (usually a good thing in France) so we sat down anyway. After a couple of minutes a short curly haired guy with a wiry moustache walked in and nodded his head to acknowledge his friends, then walked over to shake us Both by the hand *"Monsiur-Damme, bonjour"*. I tried to place him but it took a few moments to realise that he was Didier, the guy from the barber's shop just up the road. I had been for a haircut once but he wasn't very good so I hadn't been back since. He leaned against the bar but soon worked out that there was no-one there to serve him. A large bowl of oranges sat beside him and he picked one up and rolled it the three metres or so along the length of the bar. Hitting one of the bottles at the far end, the orange fell to the floor next to the table of card players. They all ignored Didier so he did it again. This time the orange was less well directed and it fell off the other side of the counter behind the bar and into a sink full of dirty glasses. There was a shattering sound and all hell broke loose. The bar's owner flung his cards to the table and, knocking his chair to the floor, leaped up and set off in pursuit of the hair-dresser. Didier had anticipated this and was already through the glass front door, which he slammed shut in the face of his pursuer. Running around the chairs and tables on the outside terrace he managed to evade capture and as the barman ran onto the road to try to gain an advantage Didier made his way back inside through the front door, which he closed and locked from the inside leaving the irate taller man shaking his fist through the large windows. We were in stitches but the rest of the men in the bar either took no notice at all or smiled meekly. "Jean-Marie and Didi have known each other from school and have played games like that ever since" explained Pascal tapping his forefinger against his temple. An enormous man with hands the size of dinner plates, we recognised him from the green-grocery stall on the Wednesday and Saturday morning markets. As we chatted to him Didier unlocked the door and Jean-Marie came back into his own bar, clipped Didi around the back of the head and sat down to resume the card game. Didier, Wendy and I had still not been served a drink. This was indeed the first of many similar encounters we were to witness in the Salamander (known thereafter as "Jean-Marie's). Pascal turned out to be a gentle giant of a man who was frequently the long suffering butt of many a practical joke. On one occasion he was standing in front of the huge plate glass window looking out at the cars going down the street when Didi came up behind him and firmly pushed him, face first into the pane. The whole room seemed to shake and I have no idea how the glass did not break. We were expecting at the very least a bloody nose but Pascal turned round, looked down at his assailant and slowly shook his head. Didi giggled like a guilty school boy. Another time Didier took his cigarette lighter and set fire to the Christmas tree which was standing next to the front door.

We were beginning to love the place and "going for the lotteries" became a ritual on Tuesday and Friday nights. Soon some of our friends started to realise we would be at the bar on those evenings. Our good pals Chris and Amanda would see us outside and would join us for a drink. They run one of the three other English owned Bed and Breakfasts in Sarlat so I suppose in a way they are our competition, but we try to help one another by passing on any enquiries we can't do to each other. We all enjoy sitting in the medieval square together on a sunny day and now we would occasionally meet at The Salamander as well. Chris is from the South West of England but despite that he is a really nice chap and one of the most generous people I have ever met. When the engine of my old car blew up Chris offered to lend me his Mercedes. I took my car to a cowboy mechanic who kept it for months but Chris was adamant that I should carry on using the Merc. At one point he knocked on our door and said "I wonder if it would be possible to borrow my car?"

Another afternoon we were in Jean-Marie's talking when a man at the next table realised we were English and we got into conversation. It turned out that David was from the Hampshire area but had lived in Sarlat for many years. We explained where we lived and that we had walked out to buy a lottery ticket and have a beer. "There is no point in me buying a lottery ticket" explained our new-found neighbour. "I'm not very wealthy but I don't have any money worries. I live in a large house with a big enclosed garden at the top of Avenue Gambetta and if I won millions of Euros I wouldn't want to live anywhere else, so what's the point?" It occurred to me that David was correct. If we hadn't started buying the tickets when we did we probably never would never have done so. As our business became more established and we became more financially secure the ridiculously small chance of winning would have seemed less of a solution to our problems. It has been said that the vast majority of tickets must be bought by the people who can least afford them, so they are in effect a tax on the poor. I understand and concur with the argument but we still enjoy buying them and who knows, one day…. David invited us to join him and his charming French wife Francoise for Sunday lunch soon afterwards and we are now firm friends. We share a love of fine wine (well, any wine actually) and good books. David is single handedly building a new wooden house overlooking the River Ceou about 20 km from Sarlat. The Ceou is a tributary of the Dordogne and I think it has the bluest water I have ever seen. David has informed me that its name is an old Occitan word for the sky and even here the sky could hardly be more pure than the colour of the water in that river. Despite the hard work and pressure I really enjoyed renovating our house and I am very jealous that David has, from scratch, designed and built his stunning new place to exactly his specification. I'd love to do that. Now, if I could only win that lottery!

Tiggy

Hi, my name is Tiggy. Well actually my full title is "Her Royal Highness Princess Tiggy of Tigglington". But you can call me Tiggy. When I was a tiny kitten I had nowhere to live. It was December and I was very cold and hungry. So I checked out tripadvisor for cats. This place called Le Jardin in Sarlat seemed to get pretty good reviews so I decided to go and live there. They have a big stone barbeque which has a chimney with a stone roof so I decided to move in there. Within a few hours a lovely lady called Wendy started to feed me. She wanted me to live in the house but there was this man called David who said it wasn't a good idea. He's never had a cat before so he's pretty stupid. He didn't even realise that cats always do exactly as they wish. Anyway I just stared at him with my big yellow eyes and *commanded him to fall in love with me. So now if it gets cold or dark I just find a nice soft cushion and have a sleep. Then they feed me. Then I explore my garden looking for dragonflies or lizards to play with. Then they feed me again. Then I climb onto the mantelpiece, have a nice scratch and snooze for the evening. Then I go to bed.*

As an example of how stupid the Davidman is: They saw a sensational Louis X1V sofa for sale at a broquant in Montignac and the Wendywoman made him buy it. For 500 Euros it was a bargain. With the addition of a 70 Euros Guy Larroche throw and two goose-feather pillows, which the Wendywoman also insisted he bought, it became possibly the most comfortable bed in history. But the Davidman didn't even realise it was for me. The next day he paid 14.99 Euros for a cat bed at the local Carrefour supermarket. What a waste of 15 quid that was! You may wake me any time after eleven in the morning. Purrrrrrrrrrrr!!!

23

Trippy

Trip Advisor seems to play an ever more important role in our business. On the whole the comparison web-site has been very beneficial to us, although at times I'm sure that everyone running a hotel or restaurant wishes at some point that it had never been thought up. It can be very rewarding to read complementary reviews but occasionally as a proprietor one has to read comments which make you doubt human nature. There is currently a restaurant in Paris taking Trippy to court hoping to obtain the right not to be on the site at all. The restaurant has a Michelin star and receives overwhelmingly excellent reviews but the proprietor/chef argues that it is just not worth spending all the hours of work necessary to monitor the site and maintain his reputation. I understand his point but there are also benefits to knowing that any client may post a review of their stay at any time. Especially for very small businesses such as ours the reviews are the only quality control system we need. Some mornings you just don't feel like cleaning a bathroom or vacuuming a carpet. You know that if you do brush up all the leaves from the front path there will be more to brush tomorrow or that if you ignore the tiny little mark that the tumble dryer has made on one of the white sheets the guests will probably never notice it. On the other hand the guests may notice any of these small things. So you clean the bathroom and vacuum the carpet. You sweep the leaves from the path and you throw the sheet that you have washed, dried and ironed back into the washing machine rather than put it on the bed. So Trip Advisor ensures that what we call "the professional standards" are maintained at all times. These are the standards that any guest would assume they would benefit from when staying at a hotel so we should certainly live up to that expectation at our Bed and Breakfast. However we also knew from the start that we wanted Le Jardin to be, if not better than, then certainly different to a hotel.

In England there used to be a perception that a B&B would be cheaper and therefore probably inferior to a hotel. There would be a stereotypically pugnacious landlady who would read a long list of rules and conditions before accepting anyone into the lodgings. "Breakfast is at 7.30 sharp so you'll be out of the house by eight and I'll not be expecting you back until 9 o'clock this evening. Lights go out at 10 and I don't want any noise after that. And don't be thinking about turning that heater on, there's no frost forecast tonight and there's a spare blanket in the wardrobe if you're cold." There would often be a snarling rottweiler at her heals just to emphasize the points made. "The room is two pounds twelve shillings and you'll be paying in advance. The bathroom is on the next landing up and if one of the other ten rooms is using it there are public toilets in the park." I once even stayed in a place like that in Bridlington and boy it was grim. There was even a toilet with just a curtain around it at the top of the stairs. I am sure that place is no longer in business because today travellers would be able to check Trip Advisor and simply would not go. Fortunately our vision for Le Jardin was somewhat different. We were both equally fed up of staying in hotels where the staff members were polite but none of the guests ever spoke to each other and the businessman on the next table would never take his eyes off his lap-top. Where the scrambled eggs for breakfast were sitting in a pool of water because they had been made an hour ago and kept warm. Where you knew that the bedroom and bathroom next door would be the same as yours because the rooms in all of this company's hotels were identical. You could be in London, Paris or New York and the hotels would be the same. So we started to look for places with a little more character and discovered some great little country house hotels. They cost a fortune but they were worth it and we realised that the smaller they were the more we liked them. So we began to try bed and breakfasts and found some little gems, firstly in the Lake District and later in Scotland, Wales and finally when we first came to The Dordogne. The thing we liked best of all in the b&bs was the contact with the owners. We got much more personal attention, advice on what to do and where to eat than we would ever get from even a very good hotel and inevitably we would be as reluctant to leave the owners as we were to leave the area where we were on holiday. Sometimes it felt like leaving friends, nowhere more so than in Sarlat, where we really did become friends with Terri, the owner of the beautiful house where we stayed whenever we came here on holiday. Then we bought Le Jardin and set up in competition to her! Remarkably she still speaks to us!

So we already had a very strong sense of the way we wanted to run our new business. That the guests would always come first and that they should feel special. That they knew we would be there if they wanted to see us but not if they wanted time alone, and that whatever they might need we would try to anticipate it. The garden would be a place for our guests to relax and the sitting room a cosy haven on cold or wet days. The guest's rooms, whilst providing everything they needed, should have charm and character. We would match the hotels for facilities and beat them hands-down for service. What we didn't know at the time was that the arbiter of our success or otherwise in this quest would be Trip Advisor. Sure we were getting great reviews, even when we first opened, but Trippy rates accommodation not just as 1 to 5 stars but also relative to other accommodation in the area. Some people find your web-site and then check your reviews, which is fine. Other people check Trip Advisor reviews for b&bs in the town and work their way down from number one. There is no point getting 5 stars if you are number 23 of 45 b&bs in Sarlat. People simply will not search that far down the page. So everything gets very competitive as each property competes to get the most 5 star reviews and improve their ranking. It's great for the guests as standards of service improve each year. For the bed and breakfast owners though, everything becomes harder as guests expect more every year.

"Do you know the number for the doctors?"

"I'll drive you there."

Or, "Is there a launderette in town?"

"Oh my washer is quiet today I'll do it for you."

So as a business you find yourself looking for ways to get an edge. We are constantly looking for further services that we can offer or added value ways to improve the rooms and garden. We thought we had a good product when we started out but, thanks to Tripadvisor (or at least because of it) we now have dozens of additions. There are cosy dressing-gowns in the bedrooms, free espresso coffee and a book exchange in the sitting-room. The swimming pool now has a sun deck with comfy loungers as well as a gazebo with a little hot-tub. We offer a different cooked breakfast every morning in addition to the large buffet choice we have always provided and sometimes even cook in the evenings if guests don't want to go out into town. All these things cost money and importantly take up much more of our time, and in reality they don't give us a huge edge over our competitors because everybody else is doing similar things. We thought we were going to be self employed but often it feels as though we work for Trippy.

The rewards, though, can be immense. The best part of our job is meeting people from all around the world and reading reviews that describe Le Jardin as "home from home" or "paradise in Perigord" really motivates us to keep improving. After six years we finally achieved a ranking of number one B&B in Sarlat and number three in Dordogne. We were even prouder when we received the Traveller's Choice", Tripadvisor's highest award. Pride comes before a fall and shortly afterwards we received our first one star review from someone who has never stayed with us. They were affronted that we asked them for a deposit to reserve a room and didn't trust them to just turn up. I know that anyone reading the review will judge it in the context of four hundred 5 star reviews, but it knocked us down to a ranking of 7th. It took us nine months to get back to number 2. Oh well, another day another Euro.

24
Guests

We often think that there is something other-worldly about our house. Our front porch is so tranquil and shaded from the heat of the sun that our guests naturally congregate to indulge in a glass of wine and to exchange accounts of their travels, their views on life in general and their personal stories.

So many people gather at about 6.30pm before they go out for dinner that we call it "happy hour". Joining them for a chat is certainly the best part of our day, and just occasionally we hear stories which make television dramas seem even duller than they actually are.

Herren and his wife Jill had been with us for four days and had three more to go before they returned to Melbourne via Bordeaux. Wends and I had been slightly confused by the fact that we were expecting newly arriving guests who had the surname Herren. We had never before heard the name, so when the two Australian couples met on our front porch we pointed out the coincidence. Apparently the guy whose first name was Herren had a Mother whose maiden name was Herren and so gave her son the "prenom" in order to perpetuate it. Are you following this? I can't remember the rest of the conversation exactly but after the two men realised they had Uncles and Aunts in common they realised that they were first cousins. There were tears and lots of hugs between the two men and the two couples went out for dinner together.

Apparently there had been some kind of family rift, and so neither knew of the others existence for over sixty years. They had come to the opposite side of the world to meet at le Jardin. They lived within 5 miles of each other and we know because of subsequent email conversations that they go out regularly together and have become firm friends.

Julie Palmer was a single traveller from New Zealand. She had been in France for a few weeks "Woofing". We had no idea what that was and I had slight doubts about whether it was legal. Working On Organic Farms is a program where people exchange labour for lodgings and Julie had been building dry-stone walls. By the time she arrived with us we were aware of the banter between Kiwis and Aussies so it was no surprise when the couple from Sydney teased Julie about being vowel challenged. "What do Kiwis have after five? – sex". " What's a Kiwis favourite supper – Fush n Chups" . You know when someone has heard a joke a hundred times before but Julie smiled and let them have their fun. Yet there is a French word which describes her in a way no English word could. Julie is a raconteur. She began by telling stories of her Uncle's roll in the Second World War. Parachuting into Italy after being shot down, he was captured and became a prisoner of war. Although badly injured he managed to escape and was found and protected by an Italian family who risked their lives to hide him in their barn. Once well enough, and given the opportunity to return to New Zealand, he chose to stay and fight in the resistance for the people who had rescued him and almost certainly saved his life. Julie had been back to Italy and she had actually met a couple of the women (now extremely elderly) who had taken care of her Uncle and remembered him. They were disappointed that he had died recently and had never come back to visit them, obviously not appreciating quite how far it is from New Zealand to Italy. Eight of us were hanging on to Julie's every word and breakfast finished at about 11.30.

The following morning she was again holding court at breakfast. Her nephew who was also her God son had been in an horrific accident. Whilst he was spraying chemicals in an attic someone had created a spark by lighting a blow torch. He was wearing trainers, a pair of shorts and a baseball cap and the attic turned into an inferno. The burns covered almost all of his body, but the soles of his feet and the top of his head at least gave some skin to transplant onto the burns. He was put into an induced coma and was not expected to survive. This young man however would not give in and surprised the medical team by determinedly fighting for his life despite a prognosis which almost certainly ended in his exit from this mortal coil. The medical staff held a meeting to discuss the options for someone who would be in agonising pain even if he cheated death by recovering from his burns. The conclusion of the meeting was that, as the young man was showing such determination to stay alive, the medical team should do everything they could to give him the chance.

At this point Geoff a young man sitting opposite Julie (a

fellow Kiwi) contributed to the story for the first time. "And how is Stephen doing now?" Julie was aware that she had not referred to her nephew by name and assumed that Geoff had read the story in the local press. "No said Geoff" "I was the lead nursing sister in intensive care when Stephen was admitted". When Stephen was eventually brought out of the coma the first words he spoke were to ask "how is my baby daughter?" she had been born, rather sickly, a week before the accident. Julie's nephew had made a full recovery after months of surgery and only the previous week had returned to work. He was still in some pain and didn't' look too great, but this time it was Julie who ended breakfast in tears of gratitude. She wasn't the only one in tears either!

Sometimes though, we end breakfast in fits of laughter. Greg and Joel were an Australian couple who had been living in London and stayed with us for a few days break before Joel had to go to New York with work. They were both really good looking lads in their early thirties and were immaculately dressed. From their manicured nails to their carefully combed hair they looked as though they could have walked straight from the pages of a fashion magazine. We were not surprised therefore when we serviced their room the next morning that everything was pristine. The bed was made just as it was on their arrival, their clothes were hung in the wardrobe in colour coordinated sets and their shirts lay in pressed piles on the shelves. Best of all though was the bathroom. Every skin and hair product imaginable was neatly standing in line on the vanity unit. The bottles in the line ran in descending height from the tallest on the left to the shortest on the right and each label faced accurately forwards. Wendy started making up stories. "I bet any money you like that they are hairdressers. Joel is probably a leading stylist at Vidal Sassoon in London. That's why he has to go to New York, their main salons are New York and London. Greg might be the assistant manager so he'll have to stay to run the London salon."

"You don't have a clue about any of this."

"I bet I'm right though. When we get to know them a bit better I'm going to find out."

So two days later at breakfast Wendy was ready to collect on her bet. "So what do you do for work Joel?"

"I work with the World Bank combating fraud and money laundering, mainly by the Chinese Triads and the Russian Mafia." The lads couldn't understand why I had just choked on my coffee and had doubled up laughing. "She had you down as a hairdresser and you're bloody James Bond!"

This wasn't the only time our guests would surprise us though. Wendy had several lengthy email exchanges with Tony who wanted to book a three night stay in October. Wendy is a good judge of character and each time Tony emailed and apologised for changing the dates they required her response got cheekier. "Now are you sure this time?" "Can I put this in my diary in ink this time because I'm wearing out my pencil?" Tony was trying to stay ahead of the joust by addressing

Wends in novel ways. "Dear Wendy Red Red Robin" "Oh Wendy Saints". So she challenged him to come up with one she had never heard before. His fifth email got close but we disqualified it as it didn't actually contain her name. "Dear Windy Day in Greendale, Elaine and I would like to bring my elderly Mother with us on the holiday. Can I book two rooms for a week?"

"Dear Postman Pat, I can do that but only with your mother's room on the second floor. Would she manage two flights of stairs?" It was not a problem as his mother played tennis every week. The conversation went on until Tony finally booked three rooms (the third for his mother-in-law) for a week at the end of October. By this time Wendy was telling him when they could come. Several more emails made their way through the ether, one explaining that Tony's mother, Penelope, was actually a Lady "But don't worry, she doesn't drive a pink Rolls-Royce". We had progressed from Postman Pat to Thunderbirds. The family excitedly arrived, all talking at once. I had looked up the correct way to address a Lady but the sprightly octogenarian held out her hand and said "Hi I'm Penny" so I never got the chance to practice. Tony had been working hard and wanted to rest and sleep for a week, Elaine wanted to see the Dordogne and go shopping and Penny and Charlotte would like a nice cup of tea. We got everyone settled with Tony and Elaine on the first floor and their respective mothers in rooms facing each other on the second. There was just one little request from Penny "Now Wendy, my dear, I usually have tea in bed at 7.30,

would it be possible for someone to bring a pot up for me?" There are tea making facilities in the rooms but we really liked her so of course, Wendy would oblige. "May I have one too?" asked Charlotte. So we set the alarm for seven, made up two trays with tea and biscuits and headed upstairs. Both bedroom doors were wide open and we could hear conversation from Penny's room, so we took the trays in there. Charlotte was sitting on the edge of Penny's bed wearing a full length satin dressing-gown; Penny quickly sat up and clapped her hands. "Oh my dears, how kind. You should just have made one pot. 'Lotte and I were just chatting. Now tell us what has happened in the world this morning. My husband worked with John Major you know, so I always like to keep up with what's going on" The next morning we would have to get up at 6.30 to swat up on world affairs. The ladies came down at a prompt 8.30 each morning and had breakfast with the Canadian couple who completed the house. All four were very genteel and polite and they enjoyed each other's company for an hour each day. Wendy and I were suitably reverential and gracious. By 9.30 the Canadians would go sight-seeing and the ladies would sit in the garden. A little later a flustered Elaine would fly down the stairs, dressing-gown and long hair flying out behind her; "Oh my darlings I'm so sorry I'm late, I slept in, what time is it, am I too late for breakfast?"
"Don't worry, you're on holiday, it's not a problem" and for the next hour we would listen to Elaine tell us about her stressful life, rebellious adolescent children, her

marital problems and her sex-life. She, like Wendy, seemed to have the ability to talk without breathing so that we could never anticipate a pause and get a word in. I think she could probably breath threw her ears like a saxophone player who can hold a note for about five minutes. My brother once saw Kenny Gee play sax and developed the hypothesis that he could breath through a different orifice altogether, but that's not for this book. We listened attentively, somewhat feigning fascination. Eventually Elaine would dash off upstairs to fetch her husband, "The poor dear has been working so hard you, know, he's exhausted, you'll have to forgive him, would he be able to perhaps just have some coffee and a piece of baguette?" Tony would sleep walk slowly down the stairs wearing a dressing gown and apparently little else. Wendy would tease him whilst he drank three cups of coffee, and worked his way through half a baguette, two croissants, and a plate of cheese and ham. By the fourth coffee he would be sufficiently awake to attempt a repost to Wendy's mocking sarcasm. "What kind of a hotel wakes you up in the middle of the night to have breakfast?"

"You'd better hurry up; you've got dinner booked for 7.30 this evening." He would go upstairs to dress at about half past eleven and we would finally get the room tidy and the dishwasher on by noon. The three ladies waited patiently in the garden. One morning after she had finished her breakfast Elaine was explaining to Wendy that she would like to go to Beynac but was not sure how to find it. Wendy explained that she would just have to follow signs towards Bergerac. "You can't miss it, it's simple", and, as Tony trudged down the stairs towards them she added "and speaking of simple". Sometimes even I don't know how she gets away with it. On the Friday evening Elaine was very excited to have discovered that the famous Saturday market was the next day and collared Wends. "You have to come shopping with me darling, we'll have such fun, I haven't had a girly day out for ages. I promise I'll get up early so we can go straight after breakfast."

"But who will make breakfast for Tony?"

"Oh don't worry darling, David can do that. Anyway if I don't go and wake him up he'll probably just sleep all day."

"Well what about your mothers?"

"They won't want to come with us!"

"That wasn't what I..."

"That's settled then, breakfast at 10, market at 10.30."

Wendy is not a great shopper but the next morning she was "doing" Sarlat market. After only a few stalls Elaine had found a dress that she coveted. "It's so reasonable darling. We're having such fun aren't we? How will I know it fits me?" Elaine spoke little French so Wendy had to ask the stall-holder. Apparently his van was parked just round the corner and Elaine could try the dress on in the back of that. "Come on Wendy, I need your opinion" So Wends found herself in the back of a wreck of an old van, sat on a wheel-arch, whilst Elaine tried on the dress. "I can't tell when I've got jeans and a jumper on" she complained and Wendy had to try to look the other way whilst she stripped to bra and knickers. Elaine is a large lady with a very ample bosom and even in the fairly large van she was struggling to get the dress on. "Help me darling, for goodness sake. It's a good job no-one can see us."

"They can, the back doors have glass windows." said Wendy, praying that no-one she knew would recognise her tugging at the back of the dress. "Oh don't be such a spoilsport darling, the worst that can happen is that he comes back to his van and kidnaps us both for ransom." Wendy either had an attack of claustrophobia or claimed that she had. Either way she was out of the van in about two seconds. All I had to do was offer Tony and the two mothers a brunch at about 1.30. The family left the next morning saying they would be back next year. "Is there any chance you could bring some day clothes next year? asked Wendy as we waved them off. A week later we received a lovely thank-you letter on House of Lords writing paper. It seemed Tony had been keeping something from us, so we emailed him. "We didn't want to be treated any differently" he replied. He didn't know us very well. He could have been the Duke of Westminster and Wendy would still have "Taken the Mickey".

25

Challenges

Nobody ever said it would be easy. Several times we have had guests tell us "we used to say we'd like to run a bed and breakfast but after watching you two for a few days we realise there is no way we could do it. We'd either kill one of the guests or each other." We've never quite done that, although once we had a guest ask Wendy "What do you do for a real job then, because this can't keep you busy?" We had just finished our two hundred and twenty third consecutive ten hour day and I was fairly certain that my wife was going to throttle her. Instead Wendy turned around and walked away, leaving me to explain that breakfasts take three hours, her admin takes at least two, cleaning another three and washing and ironing two more. Then at some point we have to do the shopping and look after the garden and pool. That's all before the most important part of our job which is spending time with our guests. "Oh I just assumed you'd finished for the day when we got up from breakfast at 9.30." Actually, once we had worked out a system we found ways to shave time from our working day. Wends sets up breakfast whilst I walk Oscar and get the bread. Then she does her admin or ironing whilst I look after the guests at breakfast. We both make the beds and clean the rooms together and if our guests are "stays" we can service the rooms in under an hour. I've even learned to hang the washing out conforming to the job specification that Wendy has set for me. I'd make somebody a lovely wife. If all goes well we can start at seven and have jobs done by 1.00p.m. If we don't have guests checking in we get the rest of the day off and we cherish the time. We can sunbathe, go for a walk, have a beer in the square or sometimes even (our absolute favourite) canoe down the river. The job can be repetitive but it means we can live in this magical place in the sun. That's not to say we don't have challenges though. The one mistake we made when renovating the house was not to use a good qualified plumber. Actually we did get quotes but they were so expensive that we settled for a cheaper solution. I could plumb all the sinks toilets baths and showers, and we knew someone who knew someone who could do all the main work and water heaters. We had been open for about two months when we first realised we might have problems. Wendy called me to say that water was dripping from the ceiling of one of the bathrooms. We had someone coming into the room that evening so I had to set about trying to find the problem. I had just about finished sealing the leaking joint when the elderly couple arrived to check in. They were exhausted by a long day travelling so they were disappointed that they couldn't go straight up to the room. Wendy explained the situation and tried to stall them until I had finished but in the end we had to ring our friend Chris who fortunately had a spare room for them. It cost us 400 Euros but that's better than having an unhappy guest. In fairness to the guy who did the plumbing we do have very hard water here and even the excellent (if expensive) plumbers that we use now have trouble from time to time. We got them to check the whole system and modify a few places where they could anticipate problems in the future. They recommended that we install a water softener so at the end of our first season we bit the bullet and coughed up the three thousand euros needed to buy one large enough for a house with five bathrooms. It certainly made a difference but we still have occasional problems with blocked shower heads and slow filling toilets.

The biggest challenges we face though are helping our guests when they have problems. A couple of times we have had guests who had been robbed before they got here. One couple arrived from Barcelona just before what little money they had left ran out. We have heard horrendous stories of pick-pockets in the city and I once witnessed it myself whilst travelling to a football match at the "Camp-Nou". I had just got on a train on the underground when there was a bit of pushing and shoving by the door in front of me. It only lasted 4 or 5 seconds but a guy got off the train just as it was pulling out of the station with three wallets and two watches. I know it is completely immoral but it was seriously impressive. I was fortunate to have been a few feet out of his grasp but our new guests had been less lucky. We spent the first day of their time with us on the 'phone to America obtaining some emergency cash for them. They were very grateful but I wasn't being entirely altruistic as we hadn't yet been paid. The second couple had been robbed in Paris. They were from Hamilton in New Zealand and arrived at our house in a state of near panic. Not only had they lost most of their money but credit cards, driving licenses and passports as well. It took us three days to arrange for replacements to be available in Paris, their next port of call, not helped by the fact that all their contacts were on the other side of the world, so the time difference was a bit of a problem. In the end we had to lend them money to get the train from Souillac to Paris.

Very often guests who have spent hours on an aeroplane develop colds or sore throats. One family, Mum, Dad, daughter and son-in-law had come to stay with us from America. The elderly father had such a bad cough that we didn't want to get too close to him. I took him to the pharmacy but they took one look and said "Get him to hospital now." After admitting him with pneumonia the doctor thought he had better examine the son-in-law, who was also coughing. He had pneumonia as well. The unfortunate two gentlemen spent their entire holiday in Sarlat hospital and I spent the week driving the two ladies back and forth to visit them.

We had another medical emergency when David and Melanie visited us for a second time. Keen motor-cyclists, they had ridden their cherished bikes from the South of England and it was obvious that Melanie was in some discomfort. She had a long-standing hernia problem and was concerned that the ride had aggravated it, so we ended up back in accident and emergency. However once she was diagnosed with acute appendicitis she was rushed to the hospital in Perigueux. The poor girl missed her entire holiday and David spent most of his riding backwards and forwards to see her and working out how to repatriate her motor-bike. On the plus side we became firm friends and we are looking forward to seeing them again this summer.

26

Satisfaction

Whatever the challenges, though, moving to France was the best decision we ever made. There are a few things we miss from England, but there are usually ways to get around any yearnings we may have. Even though I say so myself, I make great fish'n'chips and curry. Long journeys in the car are not the same without radio 2 (French radio is dreadful) but the ipod is a good substitute. We once met a woman who was going back to England because she missed buy one get one free at Iceland, and it's true that when we first came here there were very few sales or promotions in the shops. Now though there are genuine half price offers in all the supermarkets. If you see something on offer though you have to buy lots of it because it will be going back to full price the following week. We have store cupboards full of washing up liquid and dish-washer tablets. More and more we are able to buy food brands from the UK and we even have an English butcher who sells great bacon. So what do we miss? English pubs with log fires in winter. Timothy Taylor's Landlord ale (that's a personal one). The theatre and concerts, especially our favourite singer song-writer Judie Tzuke who has been touring for the last two years. Certainly not the weather! Wendy has only been back to England twice since we got here, and I've not been back many more times. To be honest even though we only go for short periods we get home-sick for Sarlat. The thing that strikes us most is the amount of traffic in England now. It was bad when we left but there is even more now. I don't know how anyone gets anywhere. Also it is only when we go back to the U.K. that we realise how clean Sarlat is. We never have litter on the streets, (although I do wish the French would clean up after their dogs) and there is no graffiti. Winter here is very quiet and some ex-pats we know like to go home or go on holiday. We have too many animals to be able to do either but we enjoy having the house to ourselves for a few months. There are always maintenance jobs to do and the garden needs tidying. We usually have a winter project too. Anyway the winters are short and we know the lovely sunny hot days will be back in April. We can get the car roof down again. It is a true delight to drive round the Dordogne as the leaves return to the trees and everything in nature looks brand new. At this time we start to look forward to seeing all our friends again. We are fortunate to have as many returning guests as we do and as they email to make reservations for later in the year we do get excited at the thought of seeing them again. Our dear friends Del and Geoffrey from Sydney come every year. Del was a famous fashion model in Australia. We're all a little older now but she is still a beautiful lady with a beautiful heart. Geoffrey is a perfect gentleman and just as importantly a member at the Sydney Cricket Ground. One of these days we will tick an item off our bucket list and watch an ashes match with them. Other friends like Cathy and Richard, Penny and Tony (who drew illustrations for this book), the Kelly family and Martin

143

and Sally are always great company and we love going out for meals with them whilst they are here. Our next door neighbours from Ripon, Angela and Ian, come out here all the time and we see as much of them now as we did whilst we lived in the U.K. We joke that we will have to go to Australia to stop them following us around. Colin and Jacqui stayed with us for four consecutive years, each time for a longer period until one year they stayed for the whole of August. Now they've bought a house here so we'll be seeing plenty of them. We love Rita and Peter and their three kids who were also regular guests, and have now bought a house in Sarlat. If any more of our guests buy houses here we won't have any customers left. They still pop round at five o'clock for happy hour though. There are many more people who have become friends after staying with us (love and apologies to all those I have not mentioned here) and that really is the most rewarding part of what we do.

I don't suppose we will ever be wealthy doing this job but we really do have the most satisfying and lovely life we could ever imagine.

Le Jardin

Le Jardin is an enchanting 200 year old house. Although very close to the centre of the beautiful medieval town of Sarlat, its garden setting will ensure a peaceful and relaxing base for your stay in The Dordogne. Please contact David and Wendy to discuss your requirements.

www.lejardin-sarlat.com

tel. +33(0)553 29 22 67

43101896R00086

Made in the USA
Middletown, DE
30 April 2017